Knitted Cushions

ALISON HOWARD

Knitted Cushions

For Kareen Dorset of the InterKnit Café in Farnham, Surrey
(interknitcafe.co.uk), who is never too busy to chat, and always
seems to know exactly what yarn to use for any project.

First published 2015 by
Guild of Master Craftsman Publications Ltd
Castle Place, 166 High Street, Lewes,
East Sussex BN7 1XU

Text © Alison Howard, 2015
Copyright in the Work © GMC Publications Ltd, 2015

ISBN 978 1 86108 776 8

Whilst every effort has been made to obtain permission
from the copyright holders for all material used in this
book, the publishers will be pleased to hear from anyone
who has not been appropriately acknowledged and to
make the correction in future reprints.

The publishers and author can accept no legal
responsibility for any consequences arising from the
application of information, advice or instructions given
in this publication.

A catalogue record for this book is available from the
British Library.

Publisher: Jonathan Bailey
Production Manager: Jim Bulley
Pattern Checker: Jude Roust
Senior Project Editor: Sara Harper
Editor: Nicola Hodgson
Managing Art Editor: Gilda Pacitti
Designer: Ginny Zeal
Photographers: Anthony Bailey and Andrew Perris

Set in Gill Sans
Colour origination by GMC Reprographics
Printed and bound in China

Why we love cushions

EVERYBODY NEEDS CUSHIONS. A ROOM JUST ISN'T COMPLETE without a few lovely squashy ones to set off a comfortable sofa or to complement a favourite armchair. Hand-knitted cushions are a favourite with top interior designers, but the downside is that they come with a hefty price tag. Fortunately, help is at hand.

The cushions in this book will give you both style and quality without breaking the bank. You can pick exactly the right yarn to suit your décor and your lifestyle, and you won't need to trail around the shops looking for what you want. Knitted cushions also make fabulous gifts that show the recipient just how much you care.

There is something in this book to suit everyone, from the beginner knitter to someone who enjoys more of a challenge, and with some different shapes thrown in for fun. There are even designs that won't cost you a penny, because you can make them from oddments in your stash. So grab some yarn and needles, cast on, and prepare to impress yourself.

Contents

9 10 11 12

13 14 15 16

25   **26**   **27**   **28**

29   **30**

If you can cast on, cast off and manage garter stitch, you can turn a simple rectangle into a cushion cover. The subtle variegated effect of the soft yarn helps to hide any uneven work.

Simply soft

Sizes
14[16:18]in (36[41:46]cm)

Tension
14 sts and 28 rows to 4in (10cm) measured over garter stitch using 6mm needles, unstretched; 14 sts and 24 rows to the same measurement stretched slightly.

Materials and equipment
Bergère de France Duvetine, 73% acrylic, 19% polyamide, 8% polyester (76yds/70m per 50g ball)
5[6:7] × 50g balls in 29090 Asperge (variegated green)
Pair of 6mm (UK4:US10) needles
Large darning needle
4 × buttons 1–1⅛in (2.5–2.75cm) in diameter OR hook-and-eye tape dots OR large press fasteners
16[18:20]in (41[46:51]cm) cushion pad

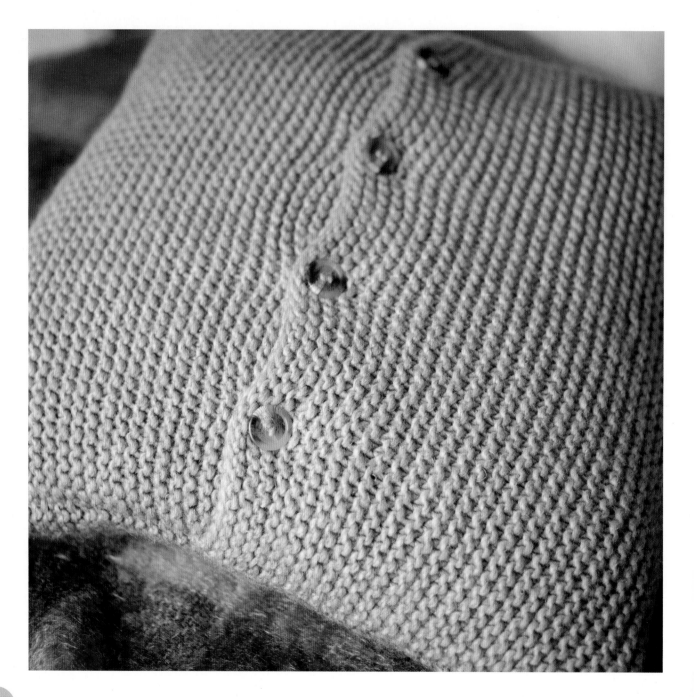

KNITTED CUSHIONS

Abbreviations

Yf = yarn forward

K2tog = knit two stitches together

Note

The cover is made in a single piece that wraps round the cushion pad. Instructions for buttonholes are given, or simply use hook-and-eye tape.

Cushion

Leaving a long end for sewing up and using the cable cast-on method (see page 137), cast on 49[56:63] sts.

Row 1: Knit all stitches.

Row 2: Slip the first stitch from the left needle to the right needle without knitting it; knit to end of row.

Repeat row 2 until work measures approx 34[40:45]in (86[101:114]cm). Follow instructions for stretching (below) as you work, and measure the length of the knitted fabric hanging from the needles rather than flat.

Buttonhole row (optional): Sl1, k7[9:12], k2tog, yf, *k8[9:10], k2tog, yf; repeat from * twice more, knit to end.

Next row: Sl1, knit to end, treating the 'yf' loops as regular stitches. Work a further 4 rows of garter stitch. Cast off loosely.

Note: You may find this easier if you use a needle a size larger for the cast-off row.

Stretching your work

As your work progresses, pull it gently downwards to ease the garter stitch slightly. As a guide, there should be about 24 rows to 4in (10cm) in length after stretching. Stretching the work will help to ensure that the cushion cover does not 'give' too much in use and become too baggy for the pad.

Making up

Lay the stretched rectangle of work flat. Measure and mark 21[24:27]in (53.5[61:68.5]cm) from the cast-on edge, making sure the markers line up on the same row of garter stitch. Fold the cast-on edge up to meet the markers on each side. Pin in place, then, working down from the markers, join each side using the garter stitch joining method (see page 149). If you find this too difficult, simply oversew the seam by picking up a stitch from one side of the work then picking up the matching stitch from the other side. Repeat until all the stitches are joined. Now fold the flap over, making sure that each side of the cushion measures 14[16:18]in (36[41:46]cm). Join the sides of the flap to the cushion cover. Attach the buttons to correspond with the buttonholes. Alternatively, attach the tape dots or press fasteners using sewing thread and small stitches.

Design note

If you haven't made buttonholes but want your cushion to look as though you have, attach a button to the right side of the flap in the same place as the tape dots or press fasteners.

Tip

Never leave your work in the middle of a row as this may pull it out of shape.

Stripes help to make a basic square look special in this
quick-to-work design. The luxurious yarn enhances
the simple but stunning effect.

Diagonal stripes

Sizes

14[16:18]in (36[41:46]cm)

Tension

15 sts and 28 rows to 4in (10cm) measured over garter stitch
using 5.5mm needles.

Materials and equipment

Artesano Aran, 50% alpaca, 50% wool (144yds/132m
per 100g skein)

1 × 100g skein in 836 Oak (brown) (A)

1 × 100g skein in 854 Birch (taupe) (B)

1 × 100g skein in 969 Ash (cream) (C)

Pair of 5.5mm (UK5:US9) needles

Large darning needle

6 × buttons ¾in (2cm) in diameter

Abbreviations

Inc1 = increase by working into the front and back of the next stitch

Ssk = slip the next two stitches, knitwise and individually, to the right needle. Push the left needle from left to right through the front of these stitches and knit them together through the back of the loops

Tip

If you are not happy about working 'ssk', just knit two stitches together through the back loops instead.

Pattern note

Break the yarn and knot in the next shade securely at each colour change. Note that the stripe pattern is worked in reverse for the flap so the stripes will match up.

Front

Using A, cast on 3 sts.

Row 1: Knit.

Row 2: Inc1, k to end.

Rep row 2 until there are 10 sts on the needle. Break off A and join in B.

Next row: Using B, inc1, k to end (11 sts).

Rep last row 7 times more.

Break off B and join in C.

Next row: Using C, inc1, k to end.

Rep last row 7 times more.

Break off C and join in A.

Cont in this way, increasing at the beginning of each row and changing colours every 8 rows, until 9 stripes have been worked.

Begin decreases. Join in next colour.

Decrease row: K1, ssk, k to end.

Rep dec row, changing colours as set every 8 rows, until 3 sts rem.

Knit one row.

Cast off.

Back

Work exactly as for front until
11 stripes have been worked.
Change yarn and work 2 rows of
garter stitch, decreasing at the
beginning of each row.
Next row (buttonholes): K1, ssk,
k5, (yf, k2tog, k6); rep instructions in
brackets to end of row.
Next row: K1, ssk, k across.
Work 4 further rows of garter stitch,
decreasing at the beg of each row.
Cast off.

Flap

Using C, cast on 3 sts.
Row 1: Knit.
Row 2: Inc1, k to end.
Rep row 2 until there are 10 sts on the
needle. Break off C and join in B.
Next row: Using B, inc1, k to end
(11 sts).
Rep last row 7 times more.
Break off B and join in A.
Next row: Using A, inc1, k to end.
Rep last row 7 times more.
Break off A and join in C.
Cont in this way, increasing at the
beginning of each row and changing
colours every 8 rows, until 7 stripes
have been worked.
Join in B and work 4 rows in garter
stitch, increasing at the beginning of
each row.
Cast off.

Making up

Place the flap on the front, wrong sides
together and matching stripes carefully.
Join using the garter stitch joining
technique (see page 149). Place the
back on the front and, matching stripes
carefully, join as far as the flap. Overlap
the last 10 rows of the back and stitch
invisibly in place carefully. Attach buttons
to correspond with buttonholes.

Variations

Work the cover in any combination of
shades, varying the width of the stripes
as you like. If you run out of yarn, you
could work the back and flap in a single
toning shade. The choice is yours, and
this project is perfect for using up
oddments of yarn.

This simple design looks impressive but can be made by a novice knitter. It is made using a strip of cream garter stitch and brown stocking stitch, and there is no need for tricky buttonholes unless you want to make them.

Half and half

Size
To fit 16[18]in (41[46]cm) cushion pad

Tension
12 sts and 17 rows to 4in (10cm) measured over stocking stitch using 6mm needles.

Materials and equipment
Rowan Purelife British Sheep Breeds Chunky (121yds/110m per 100g ball)
2 x 100g balls in 950 Bluefaced Leicester (cream) (A)
1[2] x 100g balls in 952 Midbrown Jacob (brown) (B)
Pair of 6mm (UK4:US10) needles
Large darning needle
Four press fasteners or hook-and-eye tape dots
Four buttons (any size – see note overleaf) (optional)

Pattern note

Only one ball of yarn B is needed for the smaller size if the last few rows – which will not be seen as they will be beneath the flap – are worked using yarn A.

Cushion

Using the cable cast-on method (see page 137), yarn A and 6mm needles, cast on 51[60] sts.

Row 1: Knit all sts.

Row 2: Sl1, k to end.

Repeat row 2 until work measures 16[18]in (41[46]cm).

Break off A and join in B.

Work in stocking stitch until the yarn B section measures 15½[17½]in (39.5[44.5]cm)**.

Work a further 1in (2.5cm) in garter stitch.

Cast off.

Design note

Buttonholes may be worked at ** if desired (see page 147).

Making up

Fold the cover so the beginning and end of the cream-coloured section line up, and join using the garter stitch joining technique (see page 149). Place the pad in the cover and fold the brown section over so the final 1in (2.5cm) is beneath the free end of the cream section. Pin in place and join the sides of the brown section using mattress stitch (see page 148). Line up the cream section and, working in from the sides, sew down the first 1in (2.5cm). Sew in any yarn ends. Attach buttons or position the press fasteners or tape dots and sew in place using matching sewing thread.

Tip

If you find the garter stitch joining technique tricky, oversew the seams matching the stitches carefully.

Variation

The cover can be made without any fastenings if you work an additional 4in (10cm) of the brown section and tuck it under the cream section.

Sometimes you just want something bigger, and this soft, squashy floor cushion fits the bill. The front is assembled from four diagonally worked squares trimmed with a central button.

Quarters

Size
Approx 22in (56cm) square; to fit 24in (61cm) cushion pad

Tension
9 sts and 18 rows to 4in (10cm) measured over garter stitch using 8mm needles.

Materials and equipment
Sirdar Big Softie, 51% wool, 49% acrylic (49yds/45m per 50g ball)

11 x 50g balls in 0337 Brown

Pair of 8mm (UK0:US11) knitting needles

Large darning needle

24in (61cm) cushion pad or square pillow

4 x buttons 1⅛–1¼in (2.75–3cm) in diameter

Abbreviations

Incl = increase by working into the front and back of the next stitch

K2tog = knit two stitches together

Skpo = slip one stitch, knit the next stitch, pass the slipped stitch over the knitted stitch

Sl1 = slip a stitch as though to knit it

Yf = take yarn forward between stitch just worked and next stitch

Design note

Slipping the first stitch of every row helps to produce a firm edge that will make things easier when sewing up.

Front squares (make 4)

Using 8mm needles, cast on 2 sts.

Row 1: Knit.

Row 2: K1, incl by knitting into front and back of next st (3 sts).

Row 3: Sl1, incl, k1 (4 sts).

Row 4: Sl1, incl, k to end.

Rep row 4 until there are 40 sts on the needle.

Next row: Sl1, k to end.

Begin decreases.

Dec row: Sl1, skpo, k to end.

Rep dec row until there are 2 sts on the needle.

Cast off.

Back (make 1)

Using 8mm needles, cast on 2 sts.

Row 1: K1, inc1 (3 sts).

Row 2: Sl1, inc1, k1 (4 sts).

Row 3: Sl1, inc1, k to end.

Rep row 3 until there are 80 sts on the needle.

Next row: Knit across all sts.

Begin decreases.

Dec row: Sl1, skpo, k to end.

Rep dec row until there are 41 sts on the needle.

Buttonhole row: Sl1, skpo, k5, (yf, k2tog, k6); rep to last st, k1 (40 sts).

Note: *If you prefer not to work buttonholes, simply work this row in garter stitch.*

Next row: Sl1, skpo, k to end.

Rep last row 4 times.

Cast off.

Under-back (make 1)

This is the piece that is positioned in the top right corner and is overlapped by the back. Work as for back until there are 50 sts on the needle.

Cast off.

Making up

Lay out the four squares of garter stitch and assemble into one large square using the garter stitch joining technique (see page 149); this will be used throughout. Lay the large square face down. Pin the under-back section in place and join. Pin the back section so it overlaps the under-back piece and join. Attach buttons to the under-back section to correspond with buttonholes on the back section. Alternatively, use hook-and-eye dots or press fasteners positioned inside the cover and attach decorative buttons to the outside of the back section. Attach a matching button to the centre front.

Tip

You may find it easier to use an oddment of finer yarn in a matching shade for joining.

The pattern on this cushion cover may look complicated, but after the first few rows it is actually quite simple. Choose brown or oatmeal shades to enhance the basket-weave effect.

Basket weave

Sizes

To fit 16[18]in (41[46]cm) cushion pad

Tension

20 sts and 28 rows to 4in (10cm) measured over stocking stitch using 4mm needles.

Materials and equipment

Wendy Traditional Aran, 100% wool (168yds/154m per 50g ball)

3 x 50g balls in 182 Taupe

Pair of 4mm (UK8:US6) needles

Pair of 3.5mm (UK9/10:US4) needles

Large darning needle

4–6 x buttons 1⅛–1¼in (2.5–3cm) in diameter

Abbreviations

K2tog = knit two stitches together
Yf = yarn forward

Front

Using 4mm needles and the cable cast-on method (see page 137), cast on 75[83] sts.

Row 1: Knit all stitches.
Row 2: K4, p3, *k5, p3; rep from * to last 4 sts, k4.
Row 3: P4, k3, *p5, k3; rep from * to last 4 sts, p4.
Row 4: K4, p3, *k5, p3; rep from * to last 4 sts, k4.
Row 5: Knit across.
Row 6: P3, *k5, p3; rep from * to end.
Row 7: K3, *p5, k3; rep from * to end.
Row 8: P3, *k5, p3; rep from * to end.
Rep the last 8 rows until work measures approx 15[16½]in (38[42] cm), ending on an even-numbered row.
Cast off.

Back

Using 4mm needles and the cable cast-on method, cast on 75[83] sts.
Work in stocking stitch (1 row knit, 1 row purl) until work measures approx 9½[10½]in (24[27]cm).
Change to smaller needles and work 4 rows in single (k1, p1) rib.
Cast off.

Flap

Using 4mm needles and the cable cast-on method, cast on 75[83] sts.
Work in stocking stitch until flap measures approximately 5½[6¾]in (14[16.5]cm).
Change to smaller needles and work 4 rows in k1, p1 rib.
Spread sts evenly across needles and mark the desired position of buttonholes using contrasting thread.
Row 5 (buttonholes): (Work to marker, yf, k2tog); rep to last marked buttonhole, rib to end.
Row 6: Work in rib as set.
Work a further 4 rows in rib.
Cast off loosely in rib.
Note: *If you have chosen large buttons, follow the instructions for large buttonholes (see page 147).*

Making up

Press pieces very lightly. Matching stitches carefully, join cast-on edge of back to the cast-on edge of front by oversewing from the right side. Join cast-on edge of flap to cast-off edge of the front in the same way. This will produce a firm edge with an attractive appearance. Lay joined pieces flat and pin sides of back in place. Working from the outside and using mattress stitch (see page 148), join one side of the cushion. Join the other side in the same way. Fold flap over and pin so the cast-off edge overlaps the back, approximately a third of the way down the cover. Join using mattress stitch. Attach buttons to correspond with the buttonholes.

Design note

If you are unsure what size buttonholes to make, cast on 15 sts and work a few rows, then work a sample buttonhole in either size to test which is best.

Tip

Take care when pressing the patterned side of this design or it will flatten too much.

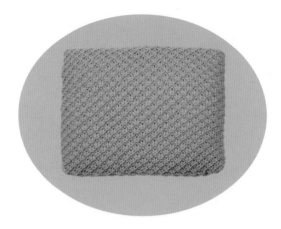

This delicate lacy design, which looks fabulous in subtle pastel shades, is created from a simple four-row pattern. The instructions can easily be adapted to make a square cushion.

Daisy stitch

Sizes

To fit 16 x 12in (41 x 30.5cm) cushion pad; instructions for a 16in (41cm) square variation are included

Tension

16 sts and 20 rows to 4in (10cm) measured over stocking stitch using 5.5mm needles, using 4-ply yarn double OR aran-weight yarn

Materials and equipment

Approx 250g of any 4-ply or aran-weight yarn in pale green

Note: 4-ply yarn must be used double

Pair of 5.5mm (UK5:US9) needles

Pair of 4.5mm (UK7:US7) needles

Large darning needle

7 x buttons ¾in (2cm) in diameter

Abbreviations

P3togWTO = purl three stitches together without taking off the needle

Yrn = yarn round needle

Design note

The design shown was worked using two strands of 4-ply wool yarn, which creates a lacier effect. Aran-weight yarn produces a pattern with slightly more definition.

Front

Using the cable cast-on method (see page 137) and 5.5mm needles, cast on 65 sts.

Pattern

Row 1: Knit all sts.

Row 2: K1, (p3togWTO, yrn, purl the same 3 sts tog again and take them off the needle, k1); rep instructions in brackets to end of row.

Row 3: Knit all sts.

Row 4: K1, p1, k1, (p3togWTO, yrn, purl the same 3 sts tog again and take them off the needle, k1); rep sts in brackets to last 2 sts, p1, k1.

Rep these 4 rows until work measures 11in (28cm).

Note: For a square cushion, work the front to 15in (38cm).

Knit one row.

Cast off loosely.

Back

Work exactly as for front until work measures 6in (15cm).

Note: For a square cushion, work back to 10in (25.5cm).

Change to smaller needles and work in k1, p1 rib for 1¼in (3cm).

Cast off.

Tip

Take care to work the stitches off in the correct order on the knit rows to maintain the integrity of the pattern.

Flap

Work as for back until work measures 4½in (11.5cm).

Change to smaller needles and work 4 rows in k1, p1 rib.

Buttonhole row: Rib 8, (yf, k2tog, rib 6); rep instructions in brackets ending last rep rib 7.

Rib a further 3 rows.

Cast off ribwise.

Making up

Do not press work. Place the front and back right sides outermost and join the cast-on edges by oversewing, matching stitches carefully. Working from the outside and using mattress stitch (see page 148), join both sides to end of ribbing. Join cast-on edge of flap and cast-off edge of front by oversewing from the outside. Join the side of the flap, overlapping the ribbing and sewing carefully in place. Attach buttons to correspond with buttonholes.

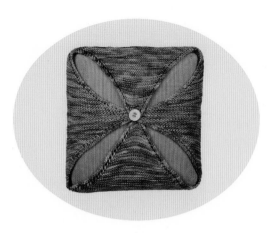

If your shabby cushion needs a facelift, this design made from a simple square covers a multitude of sins. Choose yarn that tones with the existing cover for the best effect.

Origami

Sizes

Any size – see chart overleaf

Tension

22 sts and 30 rows to 4in (10cm) measured over stocking stitch using 4mm needles.

Materials and equipment

Manos del Uruguay Silk Blend, 70% wool, 30% silk (150yds/135m per 50g skein) OR any double knitting yarn 2 x 50g skeins in 6958 Aries (variegated pinks) for a 12in (30.5cm) cushion; 3 or more for larger sizes
Pair of 4mm (UK8:US6) needles
1 x large button 1⅛–1¼in (2.75–3cm) in diameter

Abbreviations

Inc1 = increase by working into the front and back of the next stitch

K2tog = knit two stitches together

Sssk = slip the next three stitches, knitwise, and one at a time, to the right needle. Push the left needle from left to right through the front of these stitches, then knit them together through the back loops (2 stitches decreased)

Design note

This design can be made in any size; the cushion underneath is covered in a faded pink cord and was picked up for a few pennies in a second-hand store.

Preparation

Measure the width of your cushion and double it. This is the diagonal of the square that will wrap round your pad. For a 12in (30.5cm) square, it should measure about 24in (61cm). The slight overlap of the ends should stretch the cover enough to prevent it from becoming baggy.

Measuring your work

Work halfway across a row and lay the work flat, smoothing it across the needles. Pat into shape without stretching it, then measure up from the point to the needle. If you prefer to count stitches, refer to the chart below.

Cushion

Note: *If you do not want to work buttonholes, omit them and sew the points together, remembering that you will have to unpick them if you want to wash the cushion.*

Using 4mm needles, cast on 4 sts.

Row 1: Knit.

Row 2: K1, yf, k to end (5 sts).

Row 3: As row 2 (6 sts).

Row 4: As row 2 (7 sts).

Row 5: As row 2 (8 sts).

Row 6 (buttonhole): K1, yf, k2, cast off 2 sts, k3 (7 sts).

Row 7: K1, yf, k2, turn and cast on 2 sts, turn and k4 (10 sts).

Row 8: K1, yf, k to end (11 sts).

Stitch count before decreasing

Cushion size	Size of square	Sts
12in/30.5cm	24in/61cm	132
13in/33cm	26in/66cm	143
14in/36cm	28in/72cm	154
15in/38cm	30in/76cm	165
16in/41cm	32in/82cm	176
17in/43cm	34in/86cm	187
18in/46cm	36in/92cm	198

Making up

Sew in any yarn ends, weaving them carefully through the work so they do not show. Attach the button to the cast-off end of your work – that is, the point without a buttonhole. Place the cushion in the centre of the square and bring the points together, fastening them over the button.

Tip

At the halfway point of your cover, you will be able to tell how much more yarn you are likely to need.

Taking care not to pull your work lengthways, rep row 8 until work measures the same as the width of the cushion, or see chart opposite for stitch number guide.

Next row (buttonhole): K1, yf, k1, cast off 2 sts, k to last 5 sts, cast off 2 sts, k to end.

Next row: K, casting on 2 sts over each of the cast-off buttonhole sts of previous row.
Begin decreases.
Next row: Sl1, yf, sssk (to decrease by 2 sts), k to end.
Rep last row until 4 sts rem.
Cast off.

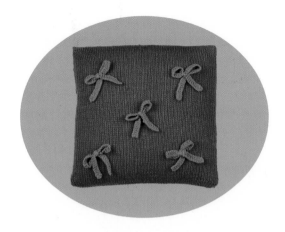

Transform a plain stocking stitch cushion cover into something truly special by adding a few narrow garter stitch knitted bows, in a contrasting colour.

Bow belle

Size

To fit 16in (41cm) cushion pad

Tension

17 sts and 22 rows to 4in (10cm) measured over stocking stitch using 5mm needles.

Materials and equipment

Drops Nepal, 65% wool, 35% alpaca (82yds/75m per 50g ball)

5 x 50g balls in 6273 Cerise

Oddment of green DK yarn

Pair of 5mm (UK6:US8) needles

Pair of 4mm (UK8:US6) needles

Large darning needle

4 x buttons 1in (2.5cm) in diameter

Method

Using the cable cast-on method (see page 137), and 5mm needles, cast on 60 sts.

Work 18 rows in stocking stitch.

Row 19: K14, p2, k28, p2, k14.

Row 20: P14, k2, k28, k2, p14.

Work 18 rows in stocking stitch.

Row 39: K29, p2, k29.

Row 40: Purl across.

Work 18 rows in stocking stitch.

Row 59: K14, p2, k28, p2, k14.

Row 60: P14, k2, k28, k2, p14.

Work 18 rows in stocking stitch.

Cast off.

Back

Using 5mm needles, cast on 60 sts and work in stocking stitch until work measures 7in (18cm).

Change to 4mm needles and work 8 rows in k1, p1 rib.

Cast off.

Flap

Using 5mm needles, cast on 60 sts and work in stocking stitch until work measures 7in (18cm).

Change to 4mm needles and work 4 rows in k1, p1 rib.

Next row (buttonholes): Rib 11, (yf, k2tog, rib 10); rep across row ending rib 11.

Work 4 more rows in k1, p1 rib.

Cast off in rib.

Abbreviations

K2tog = knit two stitches together

Ssk = slip the next two stitches, knitwise and individually, to the right needle. Push the left needle from left to right through the front of these stitches and knit them together through the back of the loops

Yf = yarn forward

Design note

The small reverse stocking stitch squares are included to set the position of the bows. Omit them if you want to make a plain cover.

Bows (make 5)

Using 4mm needles and oddment of DK yarn, cast on 3 sts.
Work in garter stitch until strip measures 12in (30.5cm).
Cast off.

Note: *You may find it easier to work the bows using short double-pointed needles.*

Making up

Press work very lightly using a damp cloth. Place the back on the front, wrong sides together, and join the cast-on edges by oversewing, matching stitches carefully. Join the sides using mattress stitch (see page 148). Position flap and join cast-on edge to cast-off edge of the front by oversewing. Join sides of flap, overlapping the rib and stitching invisibly in place. Attach buttons (which match colour of ribbons) to correspond with buttonholes. Thread cast-off end of one of the bow strips on a large needle and ease it down through the stitches on one side of the central reverse stocking stitch square and up through the other side. Repeat with remaining strips and squares. Darn in yarn ends and tie bows.

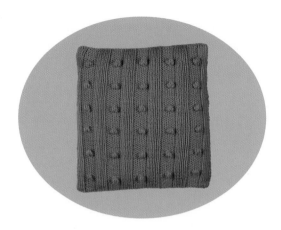

Chunky yarn knits up really quickly to produce this simply stunning cushion cover. The bobbles add extra interest and are not difficult to work once you have mastered the technique.

Bobble rib

Sizes

To fit 16[18]in (41[46]cm) cushion pad

Tension

13 sts and 18 rows to 4in (10cm) measured over stocking stitch using 5.5mm needles.

Materials and equipment

Katia Maxi Merino, 55% merino wool, 45% acrylic (137yds/125m per 100g ball)
2[3] × 100g balls in 41 Burnt Orange
Pair of 5.5mm (UK5:US9) needles
Pair of 4.5mm (UK7:US7) needles
Large darning needle
4–6 × buttons 1⅛–1¼in (2.5–2.75cm) in diameter

Tip

If your tension is the same as mine, the smaller size can be worked from two balls of the specified yarn.

Abbreviations

Sl1 = slip one stitch either knitwise or purlwise without working it

MB = make bobble: knit into front, back, front then back again of next stitch, turn; sl1, p3, turn; sl1, k3, turn; (p2tog) twice, turn; skpo

Design note

If you are worried about making bobbles, practise first using an oddment of yarn.

Cushion

Using the cable cast-on method (see page 137) and 5.5mm needles, cast on 51[60] sts.

Smaller size

Row 1: K5, (p5, k4); rep instructions in brackets to last 10 sts, p5, k5.

Row 2: P5, (k5, p4); rep instructions in brackets to last 10 sts, k5, p5.

Rep last 2 rows four times (10 rows in total).

Row 11: K5, (p2, MB, p2, k4); rep to last 10 sts, p2, MB, p2, k5.

Row 12: As row 2.

Rep rows 1–12 five times, then rows 1–10 once.

Cast off.

Larger size

Row 1: K5, (p5, k4); rep instructions in brackets to last 10 sts, p5, k5.

Row 2: P5, (k5, p4); rep instructions in brackets to last 10 sts, k5, p5.

Rep rows 1 and 2 three times (8 rows in total).

Row 9: K5, (p2, MB, p2, k4); rep to last 10 sts, p2, MB, p2, k5.

Note: When working bobbles, pull the yarn tight at the beginning of each row to avoid gaps.

Row 10: As row 2.

Rows 11–20: Rep rows 1 and 2 five times.

Rep rows 9–20 five times, then rows 1 and 2 four times.

Cast off.

Back

Using 5.5mm needles, cast on 51[60] sts.

Row 1: Sl1, k to end.

Row 2: Sl1, p to end.

Rep rows 1 and 2 until work measures 10[11]in (25.5[28]cm).

Next row: Knit across all sts.

Cast off.

Flap

Using 5.5mm needles, cast on 51[60] sts.

Row 1: Sl1, k to end.

Row 2: Sl1, p to end.

Rep rows 1 and 2 until work measures 5[6]in (12.5[15]cm).

Change to 4.5mm needles and work 2 rows in st st.

Next 2 rows (buttonholes): Mark out required number of buttonholes and work according to the size of button chosen (see page 147).

Work 4 rows in garter st.

Cast off.

Making up

With the wrong sides of the work together and matching stitches carefully, join the cast-on edge of the back to the cast-on edge of the front by oversewing. Join the cast-on edge of the flap to the cast-off edge of the front in the same way. Pin the flap in place over the back and join the sides of the cushion. Attach buttons to correspond with buttonholes.

Variation

Make the bobbles in a contrast shade, using a short length of yarn for each and sewing in the ends afterwards.

The chunky, textured pattern on this cover is produced using the cable technique, but in a slightly unusual way. The cover is made in one piece that wraps round the cushion pad.

Staggered cables

Size

To fit 16in (41cm) cushion pad

Tension

16 sts and 24 rows to 4in (10cm) measured over stocking stitch using 5.5mm needles.

Materials and equipment

Artesano Aran, 50% alpaca, 50% wool (144yds/132m per 100g skein)

3 x 100g skeins in 5167 Calder (jade green)

Pair of 5.5mm (UK5:US9) needles

Pair of 4.5mm (UK7:US7) needles

Cable or double-pointed needle

Large darning needle

7 x buttons ¾–1in (2–2.5cm) in diameter

Abbreviations

C5B = cable 5 sts back: slip next 5 sts on to a cable needle and hold at the back of work, knit next 5 sts, then knit sts from cable needle

C5F = cable 5 sts front: slip next 5 sts on to a cable needle and hold at front of work, knit next 5 sts, then knit sts from cable needle

Inc1 = increase by working into the front and back of the next stitch

Yrn = yarn round needle

Cushion

Using the cable cast-on method (see page 137) and 4.5mm needles, cast on 69 sts and work 6 rows in k1, p1 rib. Change to 5.5mm needles.

Next row (increase row): Using 5.5mm needles, (inc1, rib 2); rep to end (92 sts).

Next row: Purl.

Now work in pattern.

Cable pattern

Row 1: Knit.

Row 2: Purl.

Row 3: K1, (C5F, k5); rep to last st, k1.

Row 4: Purl.

Row 5: Knit.

Row 6: Purl.

Row 7: Knit.

Row 8: Purl.

Row 9: K1, (k5, C5B); rep to last st, k1.

Row 10: Purl.

Row 11: Knit.

Row 12: Purl.

Work in pattern until work measures

approx 31in (79cm), ending on an 11th pattern row. The piece should wrap all the way around the cushion pad.

Next row (decrease row): (P2tog, p2); rep to end (69 sts).

Change to 4.5mm needles and work 2 rows in k1, p1 rib.

Next row (buttonholes): Rib 10, (yrn, k2tog, rib 6) to last 3 sts, rib 3. Cast off.

Making up

Wrap the piece around the cushion pad, overlapping the ribbing, and tack in place. Working from the outside and using mattress stitch (see page 148), join the sides. Remove the tacking stitches. Attach the buttons to correspond with buttonholes.

Tip

The knitted fabric stretches widthwise, so do not worry if the work in progress seems too narrow.

A plain stocking-stitch cover in soft alpaca-mix yarn is transformed into something special with the addition of a pretty openwork panel and a simple lace edging in a contrasting shade.

Lace panel

Size

To fit 16in (41cm) cushion pad
Panel measures approximately 9in (23cm) square

Tension

17 sts and 22 rows to 4in (10cm) measured over stocking stitch using 5mm needles.

Materials and equipment

Drops Nepal, 65% wool, 35% alpaca (82yds/75m per 50g ball)
5 × 50g balls in 6790 Royal Blue (M)
2 × 50g balls in 6273 Cerise (C)
Pair of 5mm (UK6:US8) needles
Pair of 4mm (UK8:US6) needles
Large darning needle
9 × buttons ½–¾in (1.5–2cm) in diameter

Abbreviations

K2tog = knit two stitches together

Psso = pass slipped stitch over

Sl1 = slip one stitch knitwise to the right needle

Ssk = slip the next two stitches, knitwise and individually, to the right needle. Push the left needle from left to right through the front of these stitches and knit them together through the back of the loops

Yf = yarn forward

Front

Using M, the cable cast-on method (see page 137) and 5mm needles, cast on 62 sts.

Work in stocking stitch until work measures 15in (38cm).

Cast off.

Back

Work as for front until work measures 7in (18cm).

Change to smaller needles and work 8 rows in k1, p1 rib.

Cast off in rib.

Flap

Work as for front until work measures 7in (18cm).

Change to smaller needles and work 2 rows in k1, p1, rib.

Next row (buttonholes): K6, (yf, k2tog, k4); rep to last 2 sts, k2.

Work 5 more rows in rib.

Cast off.

Lace panel

Using C, 5mm needles and cable cast-on method, cast on 37 sts.

Work 3 rows in moss stitch (every row k1, p1 to last st, k1).

Tip

If you enjoy making the lace panel, make some more and sew them together to make a beautiful throw.

Pattern

Row 1: K1, p1, k2, (yf, ssk, k1, k2tog, yf, k1); rep to last 3 sts, k1, p1, k1.

Rows 2, 4, 6 and 8: K1, p1, k1, p to last 3 sts, k1, p1, k1.

Row 3: K1, p1, k3, (yf, sl1, k2tog, psso, yf, k3); rep to last 2 sts, p1, k1.

Row 5: K1, p1, k2, k2tog, (yf, k1, yf, ssk, k1, k2tog); rep to last 7 sts, yf, k1, ssk, k2, p1, k1.

Row 7: K1, p1, k1, k2tog, (yf, k3, yf, sl1, k2tog, psso,); rep to last 8 sts, yf, k3, yf, ssk, k1, p1, k1.

Rep these 8 rows five times more, then rows 1–4 once.

Work 3 rows in moss stitch.

Cast off.

Lace trim

Using 5mm needles and C, cast on 5 sts.

Row 1: Sl1, k1, yf, k3.

Rows 2, 4, 6 and 8: Sl1, k to end.

Row 3: Sl1, k1, yf, k4.

Row 5: Sl1, k1, yf, k5.

Row 7: Sl1, k1, yf, k6.

Row 9: Sl, k1, yf, k7 (10 sts).

Row 10: Cast off 5 sts, k to end.

Rep these 10 rows until work reaches all around the edge of the cushion cover. Place sts on a pin and do not cast off until you have sewn on the trim in case you need to work a few more rows. To cast off, work row 10 but cast off all sts.

Making up

Block pieces very lightly using a damp cloth and taking care not to stretch work. Place cast-on edges of front and back together and join from outside by oversewing, matching the stitches carefully. Repeat for cast-off edge of front and cast-on edge of flap. Join sides from outside by oversewing, and overlapping button band.

Attach buttons to correspond with buttonholes. Fit cover over pad and position panel. Pin in place, matching upright lines of work carefully. Sew in place. Beginning at one corner and leaving cast-on edge free, join lace edging to outside of cushion, sewing through the garter-stitch bumps at ends of the rows and easing round corners. Join the final 5 cast-off sts to the cast-on sts; the join should be almost invisible. Darn in ends.

The technique used for this spectacular cover is not as difficult as it looks. Add a luxurious yarn that changes colour before your very eyes and creates a bit of magic.

Entrelac

Size

To fit 16in (41cm) cushion pad

Note: *To make a cover for an 18in (46cm) cushion, cast on 56 sts and work seven triangles*

Tension

22 sts and 30 rows to 4in (10cm) measured over stocking stitch using 5mm needles.

Materials and equipment

Noro Silk Garden, 45% silk, 45% kid mohair, 10% lambswool (108yds/100m per 50g ball)

4 x 50g balls in 302 (variegated autumn shades)

Pair of 4.5mm (UK7:US7) needles

Pair of 5mm (UK6:US8) needles

Large darning needle

5 x buttons 1in (2.5cm) in diameter

Abbreviations

Inc1 = Increase by working into the front then the back of the next stitch

Ssk = slip the next two stitches, knitwise and individually, to right needle. Push left needle from left to right through front of these stitches and knit together through the back of the loops

Front

Using the cable cast-on method (see page 137) and 5mm needles, cast on 48 sts very loosely.

Work 1 row knit.

Base triangles

Foundation row: P2, turn.

Row 1: K2, turn.
Row 2: P3, turn.
Row 3: K3, turn.
Row 4: P4, turn.
Row 5: K4, turn.
Row 6: P5, turn.
Row 7: K5, turn.
Row 8: P6, turn.
Row 9: K6, turn.
Row 10: P7, turn.
Row 11: K7, turn.
Row 12: P10, turn.

Rep these 12 rows five times, ending last row p8 (six triangles worked).

First tier (edge triangles and rectangles)

Right edge triangle

Row 1: K2, turn.
Row 2: P2, turn.
Row 3: Inc1, ssk, turn.
Row 4: P3, turn.
Row 5: Inc1, k1, ssk, turn.
Row 6: P4, turn.
Row 7: Inc1, k2, ssk, turn.
Row 8: P5, turn.
Row 9: Inc1, k3, ssk, turn.
Row 10: P6, turn.
Row 11: Inc1, k4, ssk, turn.
Row 12: P7, turn.
Row 13: Inc1, k5, ssk, but do not turn.

Rectangles

Row 1: Twisting stitches to prevent gaps and working into the row end 'nubs', pick up and knit 8 sts down left side of the first base triangle, turn.
Row 2: P8, turn.
Row 3: K7, ssk, turn.

Rep last two rows to work off all sts down right side of second triangle (1 rectangle completed).

Rep instructions four times more (five rectangles completed).

Left edge triangle

Row 1: Pick up and knit 8 sts down side of last triangle, turn.
Row 2: P2tog, p6, turn.
Row 3: K7, turn.
Row 4: P2tog, p5, turn.
Row 5: K6, turn.
Row 6: P2tog, p4, turn.
Row 7: K5, turn.
Row 8: P2tog, p3, turn.
Row 9: K4, turn.
Row 10: P2tog, p2, turn.
Row 11: K3, turn.
Row 12: P2tog, p1, turn.
Row 13: K2, turn.
Row 14: P2tog, turn (1 st on needle).

Second tier (rectangles)

First rectangle

Row 1: Pick up purlwise and purl a further 7 sts down side of triangle, turn.
Row 2: K8, turn.
Row 3: P7, p2tog, turn.

Rep rows 2 and 3 until all sts have been worked off.

Second and subsequent rectangles

Row 1: Pick up purlwise and purl 8 sts down side of rectangle, turn.
Row 2: K8, turn.
Row 3: P7, p2tog, turn.

Rep rows 2 and 3 until all sts have been worked off.

Third tier (edge triangles and rectangles)

Right edge triangle

Row 1: K2, turn.
Row 2: P2, turn.
Row 3: Inc1, ssk, turn.
Row 4: P3, turn.
Row 5: Inc1, k1, ssk, turn.
Row 6: P4, turn.
Row 7: Inc1, k2, ssk, turn.
Row 8: P5, turn.
Row 9: Inc1, k3, ssk, turn.
Row 10: P6, turn.
Row 11: Inc1, k4, ssk, turn.
Row 12: P7, turn.
Row 13: Inc1, k5, ssk, but do not turn.

Rectangles

Row 1: Twisting stitches to prevent gaps and working into the row end 'nubs', pick up and knit 8 sts down left side of rectangle, turn.

Row 2: P8, turn.

Row 3: K7, ssk, turn.

Rep last two rows to work off all sts down right side of rectangle.

Rep instructions four times more (five rectangles completed).

Left edge triangle

Row 1: Pick up and knit 8 sts down side of last rectangle, turn.

Row 2: P2tog, p6, turn.

Row 3: K7, turn.

Row 4: P2tog, p5, turn.

Row 5: K6, turn.

Row 6: P2tog, p4, turn.

Row 7: K5, turn.

Row 8: P2tog, p3, turn.

Row 9: K4, turn.

Row 10: P2tog, p2, turn.

Row 11: K3, turn.

Row 12: P2tog, p1, turn.

Row 13: K2, turn.

Row 14: P2tog, turn (1 st on needle; edge triangle complete).

Rep instructions for last two tiers until 11 tiers have been worked.

Final tier (triangles)

Row 1: Cont from st left on needle, pick up and purl a further 7 sts down side of triangle, turn.

Row 2: K8, turn.

Row 3: P2tog, p5, p2tog, turn.

Row 4: K7, turn.

Row 5: P2tog, p4, p2tog, turn.

Row 6: K6, turn.

Row 7: P2tog, p3, p2tog, turn.

Row 8: K5, turn.

Row 9: P2tog, p2, p2tog, turn.

Row 10: K4, turn.

Row 11: P2tog, p1, p2tog, turn.

Row 12: K3, turn.

Row 13: P2tog, p3tog, turn.

Row 14: K2, turn.

Row 15: P1, p2tog, turn.

Row 16: K2tog, turn.

Next row: Pick up 7 sts down side of rectangle, turn.

Rep rows 2–16 until all sts have been worked off.

Cast off.

Back

Using 5mm needles cast on 60 sts and work 9½in (24cm) in stocking stitch.

Change to 4.5mm needles and work 1in (2.5cm) k1, p1 rib.

Cast off.

Flap

Using 5mm needles cast on 60 sts and work 5in (12cm) in stocking stitch. Change to 4.5mm needles and work 2 rows in k1, p1 rib. Mark position of desired number of buttonholes.

Next row: (Rib to marker, yf, work 2 sts together); rep to last marker then rib to end.

Next row: Rib across.

Work a further 3 rows in k1, p1 rib. Cast off in rib.

Making up

Place cast-on edges of the back and front together, right sides outermost. Place cast-on edge of flap to cast-off edge of the front together, right sides outermost. Pin in place then oversew. Join the sides using mattress stitch (see page 148), overlapping ribbing. Attach buttons to correspond with buttonholes. Sew in ends.

Stripes in seven vibrant shades make a design that will cheer up the dullest of days. A simple slip-stitch pattern adds extra interest to the garter-stitch stripes.

Rainbow stripes

Size
To fit 16[18]in (41[46]cm) cushion pad

Tension
20 sts and 34 rows to 4in (10cm) measured over stocking stitch using 4.5mm needles.

Materials and equipment
Bergère de France Barisienne, 100% acrylic (153yds/140m per 50g ball)
1 x 50g ball in 22306 Geranium (red) (A)

1 x 50g ball in 24936 Carotte (orange) (B)
1 x 50g ball in 24955 Tournesol (yellow) (C)
1 x 50g ball in 29039 Fenouil (green) (D)
1 x 50g ball in 29031 Azur (blue) (E)
1 x 50g ball in 22460 Pilote (indigo) (F)
1 x 50g ball in 24944 Angelite (violet) (G)
Pair of 4.5mm (UK7:US7) needles
Pair of 4mm (UK8:US6) needles
Large darning needle
6 x buttons 1in (2.5cm) in diameter

Abbreviations

K2tog = knit two stitches together
Sl1p-wise = slip the next stitch by inserting the needle from right to left
Wyb = with yarn held at the back of the work
Yb = yarn back
Yf = yarn forward

Design notes

There will be lots of loose ends on the inside of the cover, but there is no need to sew them in individually. Make sure they are knotted securely in pairs, then stroke the ends so they all lie the same way and oversew them to the inside seam.

The good-quality acrylic yarn used is available in a wide range of shades that stay vibrant after laundering. The quantity given should be enough for two cushions in the smaller size.

Front

Note: *For rainbow stripes, use the yarn in the sequence listed.*

Using the cable cast-on method (see page 137), 4.5mm needles and A, cast on 77(85) sts and work 4 rows in garter stitch.
Join in B and begin to work pattern.

Pattern

Row 1: (K3, sl1p-wise wyb); rep instructions in brackets to last st, k1.
Row 2: K1, (yf, sl1p-wise, yb, k3); rep instructions in brackets to end of row.
Row 3: Knit.
Row 4: Knit.
Join in C.
Row 5: K1 (sl1p-wise wyb, k3); rep instructions in brackets to end.
Row 6: (K3, yf, sl1p-wise, yb); rep instructions in brackets to last st, k1.
Row 7: Knit.
Row 8: Knit.
Join in D. Cont with this 8-row pattern, changing yarn colour appropriately every four rows, until work measures 15[17]in (38[43]cm).
Cast off.

Back

Work as for front until work measures approx 10[11]in (25.5[28]cm), ending on a 4th or 8th row of pattern.
Change to 4mm needles and next colour and work 5 rows in garter stitch.
Cast off.

Flap

Note: *The sequence of colours is worked backwards for the flap so the coloured stripes will match up.*

Using 4.5mm needles and the colour you were using when you cast off the front, cast on 77[85] sts and work 4 rows in garter stitch. Change to the penultimate colour and work in pattern, changing colours appropriately, until flap measures 5[6]in (12.5[15]cm), ending on a 4th or 8th row of pattern.
Buttonhole row: K10[12] sts, (yf, k2tog, k9[10] sts); rep instructions in brackets five times more, knit last st.
Change to 4mm needles and work 5 rows in garter stitch.
Cast off.

Making up

Do not press work. Place the front and back, right sides outermost, and join the cast-on edges of the front and back by oversewing, using the shade of yarn used to cast on. Join the sides of the work using the garter stitch joining method (see page 149), matching the stripes carefully. Place the cast-on edge of the flap and the cast-off edge of the front together, right sides outermost, and join by oversewing using the shade of yarn used to cast on/off. Join the sides of the flap.

Variation

This design also looks good in subtle shades of toning yarn, and would be a good way of using up oddments from your stash.

Squares in different patterns worked in oddments of toning yarn make up a cover with plenty of interest. Pop the square you are working on into your bag for the perfect portable project.

Sampler

Size

To fit a 16in (41cm) cushion pad

Tension

15 sts and 20 rows to 4in (10cm) measured over stocking stitch using 5.5mm needles;
16 sts and 21 rows to 4in (10cm) measured over stocking stitch using 5mm needles.

Materials

Artesano Aran, 50% alpaca, 50% wool (144yds/132m per 100g skein) (or similar yarn)
Oddments of cream, taupe and brown (approx 250g total)
Pair of 5.5mm (UK5:US9) knitting needles
Pair of 5mm (UK6:US8) knitting needles
Pair of 4.5mm (UK7:US7) knitting needles
4–5mm crochet hook (USG/6–H/8)
6–8 buttons
Large darning needle

Abbreviations

CIF = cable 1 st forward, either in the normal way (see page 142) or by knitting into the back of the second st on the left needle, then into the front of the first st

Note: The squares are made using a different number of stitches depending on how much the stitch pulls in.

Front

Using 5mm needles and selecting from the patterns given, make a total of 9 squares. The design shown uses one baby cable square surrounded by two squares each of basket stitch, moss stitch, mistake rib and garter stitch. Use two colours for the squares, reserving the darkest for the criss-cross lines.

Patterns

Basket weave

Cast on 20 sts.

Row 1: P3, (k2, p4); rep to last 5 sts, k2, p3.

Row 2: K3, (p2, k4); rep to last 5 sts, p2, k3.

Row 3: Knit.

Row 4: Purl.

Row 5: (K2, p4); rep to last 2 sts, k2.

Row 6: (P2, k4); rep to last 2 sts, p2.

Tip

Substitute any of your favourite patterns for those shown, checking tension carefully.

Row 7: (K2, p4); rep to last 2 sts, k2.
Row 8: (P2, k4); rep to last 2 sts, p2.
Row 9: Knit.
Row 10: Purl.
Row 11: As row 1.
Row 12: As row 2.
Rep from row 1 until work measures approx 5in (12.5cm) ending on 6th row of pattern.
Cast off.

Baby cable

Cast on 22 sts.
Row 1: (P2, k2); rep to last 2 sts, p2.
Row 2: (K2, p2); rep to last 2 sts, k2.
Row 3: (P2, C1F) to last 2 sts, p2.
Row 4: As row 2.
Rep these 4 rows until work measures approx 5in (12.5cm).
Cast off.

Garter stitch

Cast on 19 sts.
Work until piece measures approx 5in (12.5cm), slightly stretched.
Cast off.

Moss stitch

Cast on 19 sts.
Row 1: (K1, p1); rep to last st, k1.
Rep this row until work measures approx 5in (12.5cm).
Cast off.

Mistake rib

Cast on 21 sts.
Row 1: (K2, p2); rep to last st, k1.
Rep this row until work measures approx 5in (12.5cm).
Cast off.

Back

Using 5.5mm needles, cast on 56 sts. Work in two-row stripes in stocking stitch for 9in (23cm).
Change to 4.5mm needles and work 8 rows in k1, p1 rib in a single shade.
Cast off in rib.

Flap

Using 5.5mm needles, cast on 56 sts. Working in stripes as before, work 4½in (11.5cm) in stocking stitch.
Change to 4.5mm needles and work 2 rows in k1, p1 rib.
Mark position of buttonholes.
Next row (buttonholes): (Rib to marker, yf, k2tog); rep to last marker, yf, k2tog, rib to end.
Next row: Rib.
Work 4 further rows in rib.
Cast off in rib.

Contrast trim

Using the crochet hook and the darkest shade of yarn, work 4 x 16in (41cm) lengths of chain stitch. Fasten off, leaving a long end for sewing on the chain.
Note: *If you cannot crochet, make 4 x 16in (41cm) plaits using three strands of yarn.*

Making up

Arrange the squares as required and join by oversewing. Place the strands of contrast trim over the joins and attach using backstitch (see page 149). Tack the back and flap in place, wrong sides of work together and overlapping the button band. Join the edges of the cover using mattress stitch (see page 148). Attach buttons. Darn in yarn ends.

Soft pink merino wool makes a cushion fit to grace the boudoir of any princess. The smocking can be worked either by sewing or, for more experienced knitters, as part of the design.

Smocked

Size

To fit a 16in (41cm) cushion pad

Tension

22 sts and 30 rows to 4in (10cm) measured over stocking stitch using 4.5mm needles.

Materials

Katia Merino, 100% superwash merino wool (111yds/102m per 50g ball)

5 x 50g balls in 007 Pale Pink

Pair of 4.5mm (UK7:US7) knitting needles

Pair of 3.5mm (UK9/10:US4) knitting needles

Large darning needle

Short double-pointed needle (dpn)

5–6 x buttons 1in (2.5cm) in diameter

Front

Using 4.5mm needles and the cable cast-on method (see page 137), cast on 91 sts.

Row 1 (WS): K3, (p1, k3); rep to end.
Row 2 (RS): P3, (k1, p3); rep to end.
Rep these 2 rows until 112 rows have been worked and piece measures approx 15in (38cm).
Cast off.

Back

Using 4.5mm needles, cast on 84 sts.
Work in stocking stitch until work measures 7in (18cm).
Change to 3.5mm needles and work 8 rows in k1, p1 rib.
Cast off in rib.

Flap

Using 4.5mm needles, cast on 84 sts.
Work in stocking stitch until work measures 7in (18cm).
Change to 3.5mm needles and work 2 rows in k1, p1 rib.
Mark position of desired number of buttonholes.

Next row (buttonholes): Work to first marker, (cast off 2 sts, work to next marker); rep to last marker, cast off 2 sts, work to end.

Next row: Rib, casting on 2 sts over cast-off sts on previous row.
Work 4 rows in rib.
Cast off in rib.

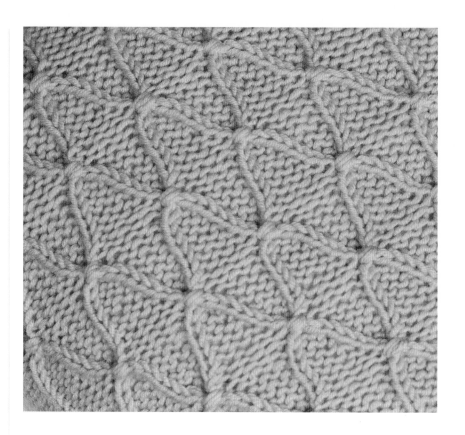

Smocking
First tier

With RS of the front facing and using a length of yarn measuring about 50in (127cm), count to the 8th stitch up on first line of ribbing and join to the 8th stitch up on second line of ribbing by oversewing three or four times. Fasten off at back and take yarn loosely across to the 8th stitch up on third line of ribbing, then join to the 8th stitch up on fourth row of ribbing in same way. Continue across row and fasten off.

Second tier

With RS of front facing and using a length of yarn measuring about 50in (127cm), count to the 8th stitch up from the first tier of smocking on the second line of ribbing and join to the 8th stitch up from the first tier of smocking on the third line of ribbing by oversewing. Fasten off at back and take yarn loosely across to the 8th stitch up on the fourth line of ribbing, then join to the 8th stitch up from the first tier of smocking on the fifth row of ribbing.

Continue across the row and fasten off. Repeat over the whole front, counting up 8 sts for every tier and alternating the stitches joined to produce the smocked effect.

Making up

Do not press work. Place the front and back, right sides outermost, and join the cast-on edges by oversewing. Join sides of work using mattress stitch (see page 148) to end of ribbed section. Place cast-on edge of flap and cast-off edge of front together with right sides outermost, and join by oversewing. Join sides of flap to sides of front, overlapping the button band. Attach the buttons to correspond with buttonholes. Sew in ends.

(see page 148)

(see page 137)

> ## Tip
>
> *For a different effect, work the smocked ties in contrasting yarn.*

Variation

As an alternative, the smocking can be worked as part of the design by using a knitted tie. Follow these instructions if you wish to do this.

Abbreviation

Tie = slip next 5 sts on to a dpn. Wind the yarn, anti-clockwise, three times around these sts, then work them off as k1, p3, k1

Alternative front (knitted-in ties)

Using 4.5mm needles and the cable cast-on method (see page 137), cast on 91 sts.

Rows 1, 3, 5 and 7: K3, (p1, k3); rep to end.

Rows 2, 4 and 6: P3, (k1, p3); rep to end.

Row 8: P3, (tie over 5 sts, p3); rep to end.

Rows 9, 11, 13 and 15: As row 1.

Rows 10, 12 and 14: As row 2.

Row 16: P3, k1, p3, (tie over 5 sts, p3); rep to last 4 sts, k1, p3. Rep these 16 rows until work measures 15in (38cm). Cast off.

A visit to an art gallery provided the inspiration for this striking cushion cover worked in simple stocking stitch. Vary the shades to suit your décor, or use up oddments from your stash.

Modern art

Size
To fit a 16in (41cm) cushion pad

Tension
22 sts and 28 rows to 4in (10cm) measured over stocking stitch using 4mm needles.

Materials and equipment
Inti Alpaca Select, 50% alpaca, 50% acrylic (115yds/105m per 50g ball)
2 x 50g balls in 004 Chocolate (A)

Debbie Bliss Blue-faced Leicester DK, 100% wool (118yds/108m per 50g ball)
1 x 50g ball in 46509 Fuchsia (B)
1 x 50g ball in 46501 Ecru (C)
1 x 50g ball in 46507 Burnt Orange (D)
Pair of 4mm (UK8:US6) needles
Pair of 3.5mm (UK9/10:US4) needles
Large darning needle
8 x buttons 1in (2.5cm) in diameter

Abbreviations

Yf = take yarn forward between stitch just worked and next stitch

Yrn = yarn round needle (when yarn is in purl position)

Front

Using A, 4mm needles and cable cast-on method (see page 137), cast on 78 sts and work 2 rows in stocking stitch.
Break off A, join in B and work 32 rows in stocking stitch.

Break off B, join in A and work 2 rows in stocking stitch.
Break off A, join in C and work 32 rows in stocking stitch.
Break off C, join in A and work 2 rows in stocking stitch.
Break off A, join in D and work 32 rows in stocking stitch.
Break off D, join in A and work 2 rows in stocking stitch.
Cast off.

Front edges

With RS facing and using A, pick up and knit 84 sts along the right edge of front (approx 3 sts for every 4 rows). Beginning with a purl row, work 2 rows in stocking stitch.

Cast off.

With RS facing and using A, pick up and knit 84 sts along the left edge of front (approx 3 sts for every 4 rows). Beginning with a purl row, work 2 rows in stocking stitch.

Cast off.

Lower back

Using A, 4mm needles and the cable cast-on method, cast on 84 sts. Work in stocking stitch until work measures 9in (23cm).

Change to 3.5mm needles and work in k1, p1 rib for 1in (2.5cm).

Cast off in rib.

Upper back

Using A, 4mm needles and the cable cast-on method, cast on 84 sts. Work in stocking stitch until work measures 5in (12.5cm).

Change to 3.5mm needles and work 2 rows in k1, p1 rib.

Next row (buttonholes): Rib 10, (yf, k2tog, rib 7, yrn, p2tog, rib 7); rep instructions in brackets to last 2 sts, k2.

Making up

Press work very lightly. With right sides outermost, join cast-on edge of front to cast-on edge of lower back by oversewing, matching the stitches carefully. Join cast-off edge of front to cast-on edge of upper back in same way. Overlapping the button band, join sides by oversewing. Attach buttons to correspond with buttonholes.

A clever technique makes a patchwork-effect design that needs no fiddly sewing up – and there are no complicated fastenings either. Use at least four colours so they never overlap.

Easy patchwork

Size

To fit 16in (41cm) cushion pad
Use a pad with synthetic filling if you want to wash the cushion, as the cover is sewn on the pad

Tension

16 sts and 24 rows to 4in (10cm) measured over stocking stitch using 5.5mm needles.

Materials and equipment

Artesano Aran, 50% alpaca, 50% wool (144yds/132m per 100g skein)
1 × 100g skein in C836 Oak (dark brown)
1 × 100g skein in C859 Walnut (mid-brown)
1 × 100g skein in C854 Birch (light brown)
1 × 100g skein in CA03 Maple (cream)
Pair of 5.5mm (UK5:US9) needles
Pair of 5mm (UK6:US8) needles
Large darning needle

Pattern note

Begin with any shade of yarn and use a different shade for each of the first four sections. For the fifth section, use the third shade again and for the sixth section use the first shade again. Work the seventh section using the second shade, the eighth using the first shade and the ninth using the fourth shade. For a larger cover, to fit a 19–20in (48.5–51cm) pad, work two extra sections in the same way, using the third and the fourth shades and taking the final stitch count to 72.

Front and back

Make two alike or using a different sequence of shades.

Note: *The smaller needles are used throughout for picking up stitches.*

First section

Using 5.5mm needles and shade 1, cast on 12 sts and knit 20 rows.

Cast off 11 sts.

Break off yarn and join in shade 2.

Second section

Using a 4.5mm needle, knit the last stitch of the previous section. Rotate piece anti-clockwise and pick up 11 sts down left side of first square (12 sts). Using 5.5mm needles, work 19 rows in garter stitch.

Cast off 11 sts.

Break off yarn and join in shade 3.

Third section

Using a 4.5mm needle, knit last stitch. Rotate piece as before and pick up 23 sts down left side of work (24 sts). Using 5.5mm needles, work 19 rows in garter stitch.

Cast off 23 sts.

Break off yarn and join in shade 4.

Fourth section

Using a 4.5mm needle, knit last stitch. Rotate piece as before and pick up 23 sts down left side of work (24 sts). Using 5.5mm needles, work 19 rows in garter stitch.

Cast off 23 sts.

Break off yarn and join in shade 3.

Fifth section

Using a 4.5mm needle, knit last stitch. Rotate piece as before and pick up 35 sts down left side of work (36 sts). Using 5.5mm needles, work 19 rows in garter stitch.

Cast off 35 sts. Break off yarn and join in shade 1.

Sixth section

Using a 4.5mm needle, knit last stitch. Rotate piece as before and pick up 35 sts down left side of work (36 sts). Using 5.5mm needles, work 19 rows in garter stitch.

Cast off 35 sts. Break off yarn and join in shade 2.

Seventh section

Using a 4.5mm needle, knit last stitch. Rotate piece as before and pick up 47 sts down left side of work (48 sts). Using 5.5mm needles, work 19 rows in garter stitch.

Cast off 47 sts. Break off yarn and join in shade 1.

Eighth section

Using a 4.5mm needle, knit last stitch. Rotate piece as before and pick up 47 sts down left side of work (48 sts). Using 5.5mm needles, work 19 rows in garter stitch.

Cast off 47 sts. Break off yarn and join in shade 4.

Ninth section

Using a 4.5mm needle, knit last stitch. Rotate piece as before and pick up 59 sts down left side of work (60 sts). Using 5.5mm needles, work 19 rows in garter stitch.

Cast off.

Making up

Darn in yarn ends. Place the two pieces of the cover together, right sides outermost and pin in place. Join three of the sides using the garter stitch joining technique where appropriate (see page 149), and mattress stitch for other seams (see page 148). Insert cushion pad and join final seam.

Just one ball of super-chunky yarn makes a gorgeous design that grows quickly and could be the bargain of the century. Contrasting edging and a big button add to its striking looks.

Big envelope

Size

To fit an 18in (46cm) pad

Tension

10 sts and 14 rows to 4in (10cm) measured over stocking stitch using 8mm needles.

Materials and equipment

Robin Candyfloss, 100% acrylic (306yds/280m per 200g ball)
1 x 200g ball in 4454 Big Dipper (variegated pinks, blues, greens and yellows)
Pair of 8mm (UK0:US11) knitting needles
Large darning needle
1 x button 1¾in (4.25cm) in diameter

Abbreviations

Ssk = slip the next two stitches, knitwise and individually, to the right needle. Push the left needle from left to right through the front of these stitches and knit them together through the back of the loops

Back

Using 8mm needles and cable cast-on method (see page 137), cast on 44 sts. Work in stocking stitch until work measures 16½in (42cm).
Cast off loosely.

Front

Using 8mm needles and the cable cast-on method, cast on 44 sts. Work in stocking stitch until work measures 17in (43cm), ending with a purl row.

Decrease for flap:
Row 1: Ssk, k to last 2 sts, k2tog.
Row 2: K1, p to last st, k1.
Rep the last 2 rows until 14 sts rem.
Next row (buttonhole): Ssk, k3, cast off 4 sts, k3, k2tog.
Next row: Purl, casting on 4 sts over cast-off sts of previous row.
Next row: Ssk, k to last 2 sts, k2tog.
Next row: Purl.
Cont in this way until there are 6 sts on the needle.
Purl one row.

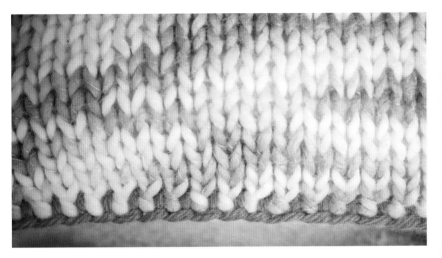

Increase for under-flap:

Next row: Inc in first st, k to last st, inc in last st.

Next row: Purl.

Cont in this way until there are 12 sts on the needle.

Next row (buttonhole): Inc1, k3, cast off 4 sts, k3, inc1.

Next row: Purl, casting on 4 sts over 4 cast-off sts of previous row.

Next row: Inc1, k to last st, inc1.

Next row: Purl.

Cont in this way until there are 44 sts on the needle.

Break off yarn and run through sts. Fasten off.

Making up

Press pieces very lightly using a damp cloth and a cool iron. Assemble the pieces wrong sides together, and tack very carefully in place. Line up inside flap and sew in place on reverse of work, keeping the stitches loose so they do not show on the right side. Using a double strand of contrast yarn, and beginning at one side of the flap, work blanket stitch (see page 150) around entire edge of cushion, flap and along the top (inside) edge of the front. Using a single strand of the main yarn, oversew the edges of the buttonholes together. Insert cushion pad and attach the button halfway down the centre front of cover. When you are happy with the effect, sew the top edges of the flap in place so they do not gape when the cushion is in use.

A two-colour pattern gives the front of this cover an interesting texture, while striking buttons make a feature of the plain back. Vary the shades used to match your décor.

Corn cob

Size

To fit 16in (41cm) cushion pad

Tension

17 sts and 22rows to 4in (10cm) measured over stocking stitch using 5mm needles.

Materials and equipment

Drops Alaska, 100% wool (77yds/70m per 50g ball)

2 × 50g balls in 45 Light Olive (M)

2 × 50g balls in 58 Mustard (C)

Pair of 7mm (UK2:US10.5) needles

Pair of 5mm (UK6:US8) needles

Pair of 4mm (UK8:US6) needles

Large darning needle

5 × buttons 1⅛–1¼in (2.5–3cm) in diameter

Abbreviations

K1b = knit into the back of the stitch

K2tog = knit two stitches together

Sl1wyb = slip one stitch with yarn held at the back of the work

Yb = yarn back

Yf = yarn forward

Pattern note

Larger needles are used for the patterned front because the work pulls in quite tightly. When working this pattern, you will always be slipping the stitch in the opposite colour to the one in use.

Front

Using M, the cable cast-on method (see page 137) and 7mm needles cast on 60 sts. Knit one row, then change to C and begin to work in pattern. Do not break off M; carry yarn not in use up side of work.

Corn cob pattern

Row 1: Using C, k1, (k1b, sl1wyb); rep to last st, k1.

Row 2: Using C, k1, (yf, sl1, yb, k1); rep to last st, k1.

Row 3: Using M, k1, (sl1wyb, k1b); rep to last st, k1.

Row 4: Using M, k1, (k1, yf, sl1, yb); rep to last st, k1.

Rep these 4 rows until work measures 15in (38cm) from beginning.

Cast off.

Back

Using 5mm needles and M, cast on 60 sts and work 9in (23cm) in stocking stitch.

Change to 4mm needles and work 6 rows in k2, p2 rib thus: p1, k2, p2, ending k1.

Cast off.

Flap

Using 5mm needles and M, cast on 60 sts and work 6in (15cm) in stocking stitch.

Change to 4mm needles and work 2 rows in k2, p2 rib thus: p1, k2, p2, ending k1.

Next row (buttonholes): Rib 9, (cast off 3 sts, rib 7); rep to last st, k1.

Next row: Work in rib, casting on 3 sts over each set of 3 sts cast off on previous row.

Work 5 further rows in rib.

Cast off.

Making up

Block back and flap very lightly. Join using mattress stitch (see page 148), overlapping bands. Darn in the ends. Attach buttons to correspond with the buttonholes.

Tip

If the edges of the patterned front look a little 'frilly', run a gathering thread down the sides to straighten them before joining the pieces.

A traditional pattern of twisted stitches adds interest to this design in reverse stocking stitch. It is not for the faint-hearted, but the results are well worth the effort.

Entwined trees

Size

To fit 16in (41cm) cushion pad

Tension

17 sts and 21 rows to 4in (10cm) measured over stocking stitch using 5mm needles.

Materials and equipment

Artesano Aran, 50% alpaca, 50% wool (144yds/132m per 100g ball)

4 x 100g balls in C859 Walnut (brown)

Pair of 5mm (UK6:US8) needles

Pair of 4mm (UK8:US6) needles

Large darning needle

Cable needle (CN)

6 x buttons 1in (2.5cm) in diameter

Abbreviations

K1b = knit into the back of the stitch

M1 = make one stitch by picking up the strand of yarn between the last stitch worked and the next stitch and knitting into the back of it

Ssk = slip the next two stitches, knitwise and individually, to the right needle. Push the left needle from left to right through the front of these stitches and knit them together through the back of the loops

Cable stitches key

C1F = slip 1 st to CN and hold at front, p1, k1 from CN

C1B = slip 1 st to CN and hold at back, k1, p1 from CN

C2FP = slip 2 sts to CN and hold at front, p2, k2 from CN

C2BP = slip 2 sts to CN and hold at back, k2, p2 from CN

C2FK = slip 2 sts to CN and hold at front, k2, k2 from CN

C2BK = slip 2 sts to CN and hold at back, k2, k2 from CN

C2/1F = slip 2 sts to CN and hold at front, p1, k2 from CN

C2/1B = slip 1 st to CN and hold at back, k2, p1 from CN

Note: The stitch count increases to accommodate the gathering effect of the cables, then decreases again.

Front

Using the cable cast-on method (see page 137), cast on 62 sts and, beginning with a purl row, work 12 rows in stocking stitch.
Set position of pattern.

(see page 137)

Tip

If you make a plain back without fastenings and sew the pad into the cushion cover, you can make this cushion using just two skeins of the specified yarn.

Tree pattern

Row 1 (WS): K23, p4, k8, p4, k23.

Row 2: P23, k4, p8, k4, p23.

Keeping to pattern as set, work a further 13 rows.

Row 16: P23, M1, k4, p8, k4, M1, p23 (64 sts).

Row 17: K23, p5, k8, p5, k23.

Row 18: P23, k1, M1, k4, p8, k4, M1, k1, p23 (66 sts).

Row 19 and rem alt rows: Knit or purl stitches appropriately as they present.

Row 20: P21, C2BP, k4, M1, p8, M1, k4, C2FP, p21 (68 sts).

Row 22: P19, C2BP, p2, k4, M1, k1, p8, k1, M1, k4, p2, C2FP, p19 (70 sts).

Row 24: P17, C2BP, p4, k4, C2FP, p4, C2BP, k4, p4, C2FP, p17.

Row 26: P16, C2/1B, p5, C2/1B, k2, p2, C2FP, C2BP, p2, k2, C2/1F, p5, C2/1F, p16.

Row 28: P16, k2, p5, C2/1B, p1, C2/1F, p3, p3, C2/1B, p1, C2/1F, p5, k2, p16.

Row 30: P15, C1B, C1F, p3, C2/1B, p3, C2/1F, C2BP, C2FP, C2/1B, p3, C2/1F, p3, C1B, C1F, p15.

Row 32: P14, C1B, p2, k1B, p3, k2, p5, C2FK, p4, C2BK, p5, k2, p3, k1B, p2, C1F, p14.

Row 34: P13, (C1B, P2) twice, C1B, C1F, p3, C2/1B, C2/1F, p2, C2/1B, C2/1F, p3, C1B, (C1F, p2) twice, C1F, p13.

Row 36: P16, (C1B, p2) twice, k1B, p3, k2, p2, C2/1F, C2/1B, p2, k2, p3, k1B, (p2, C1F) twice, p16.

Row 38: P15, (C1B, p2) three times, C1B, C1F, p2, C2FK, p2, C1B, (C1F, p2) 3 times, C1F, p15.

Row 40: P14, C1B, p6, (C1B, p2) twice, k1B, p2, k4, p2, k1B, (p2, C1F) twice, p6, C1F, p14.

Row 42: P13, p2tog, p6, (C1B, p2) 3 times, C2FK, (p2, C1F) 3 times, p6, p2tog, p13 (68 sts).

Row 44: P19, C1B, p6, C1B, p1, C2BP, C2FP, p1, C1F, p6, C1F, p19.

Row 46: P18, p2tog, p6, C1B, p1, C1B, C1F, p2, C1B, C1F, p1, C1F, p6, p2tog, p18 (66 sts).

Row 48: P24, C1B, p1, C1B, p2, k1B, p2, k1B, p2, C1F, p1, C1F, p24.

Row 50: P23, p2tog, p1, (C1B, p2) twice, C1F, p2, C1F, p1, p2tog, p23 (64 sts).

Row 52: P24, p2tog, p2, C1B, p4, C1F, p2, p2tog, p24 (62 sts).

Row 54: P27, k1b, p6, k1b, p27.

Row 56: P27, p2tog, p4, p2tog, p27 (60 sts).

Work in stocking stitch until work measures 15½in (39.5cm).

Cast off.

Back

Using 5mm needles, cast on 62 sts and, beginning with a purl row, work in stocking stitch for 10in (25.5cm).

Change to 4mm needles and work 6 rows in k1, p1 rib.

Cast off in rib.

Flap

Work as back until piece measures 4in (10cm).

Change to 4mm needles and work 2 rows in k1, p1 rib.

Next row (buttonholes): Rib 10, k2tog, yf, (rib 6, k2tog, yf) 5 times, rib 10.

Work 3 further rows in rib.

Cast off in rib.

Making up

Place the cast-on edges of the front and back together, wrong side outermost, and join by oversewing. Repeat with the cast-on edge of the flap and the cast-off edge of the front. Turn the cover right side out and fit around the cushion pad, overlapping the button band and tacking the flap in place temporarily. Join the sides from the outside using the garter stitch joining technique (see page 149). Remove tacking stitches. Attach buttons to correspond with the buttonholes. Attach tassels if liked.

Tassels

Cut 48 lengths of yarn about 9in (23cm) long. Follow the method given on page 150 to produce four tassels, each using 12 lengths of yarn.

A plain cover becomes interesting with contrasting stripes of variegated yarn, sewn together to form ridges. For those with more confidence, a method of knitting in the ridges is also given.

Ridges

Sizes

To fit 16[18]in (41[46]cm) cushion pad

Tension

22 sts and 30 rows to 4in (10cm) measured over stocking stitch using 4mm needles.

Materials and equipment

Jarol Heritage Classic DK, 55% wool, 25% acrylic, 20% nylon (267yds/245m per 100g ball)
2 × 100g balls in 107 Lilac (M)
King Cole Riot DK, 30% wool, 70% acrylic (324yds/294m per 100g ball)
1 × 100g ball in 400 Spirit (variegated navy/dark red) (C)
Pair of 4mm (UK8:US6) knitting needles
Pair of 3.25mm (UK10:US3) knitting needles
Large darning needle

Front
Method 1 (sewn ridges)

Using the cable cast-on method (see page 137), 4mm needles and M, cast on 82[90] sts.

Work 6 rows in stocking stitch.

Change to C and work 6 rows in stocking stitch.

Change to M and work 6 rows in stocking stitch.

Cont in this way until 14[16] contrast stripes and 15[17] sections of M yarn have been worked.

Cast off.

Thread darning needle with M yarn and, working from the back, join the first stitch of the first contrast stripe to the corresponding stitch 6 rows above. Repeat across row to form ridge.

Join every contrast stripe in the same way to form ridges.

Method 2 (knitted-in ridges)

Using the cable cast-on method, 4mm needles and M, cast on 82[90] sts.

Work 6 rows in stocking stitch.

*Change to C and work 6 rows in stocking stitch.

Change to M and work across row, knitting each stitch together with the C stitch 6 rows below.

Work 5 further rows in M.

Rep from * until 14[16] ridges and 15[17] sections of M yarn have been worked.

Cast off.

Back pieces (make 2)

Using the cable cast-on method, 4mm needles and M, cast on 82[90] sts.

Work in stocking stitch for 9½[11]in (24[28]cm).

Change to smaller needles and work ½in (1cm) in k1, p1 rib.

Cast off in rib.

Making up

Place the front and one of the back pieces together, right sides outermost. Join the cast-on edges together by oversewing. Pin the ribbing of the back to the front, making sure that it lines up with a ridge. Join the sides using mattress stitch (see page 148), making sure that each ridge is smoothed downwards as you join the work. Place the cast-off edge of the front and the cast-on edge of the second back piece together and join by oversewing. Pin the second back piece in place, overlapping the first and making sure the ribbing lines up. Join using mattress stitch, overlapping the first back piece. Sew in yarn ends.

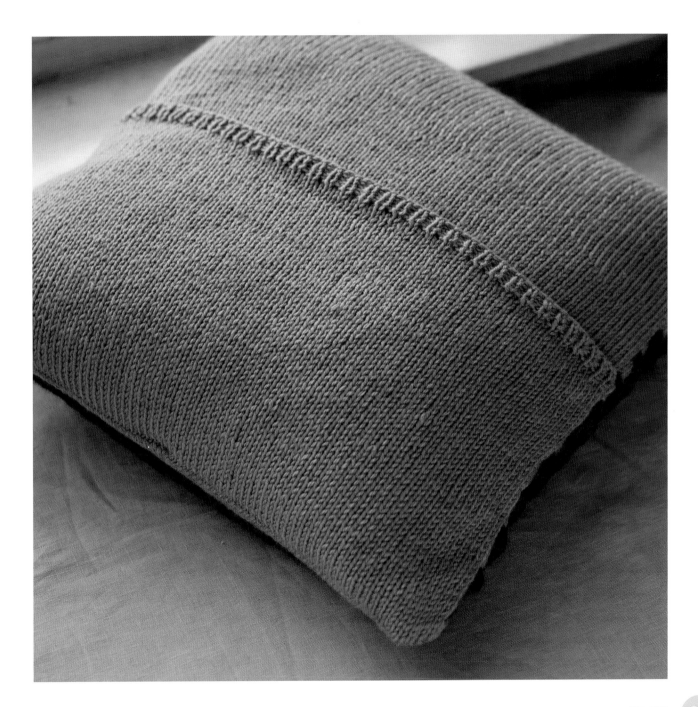

This cover, inspired by a traditional Danish design, conjures up thoughts of cold winter nights. The chosen yarn comes in a huge range of colours so the combinations can be varied to suit your taste.

Snowflake

Size

To fit a 16in (41cm) cushion pad

Tension

17 sts and 21 rows to 4in (10cm) measured over stocking stitch using 5mm needles.

Materials

Artesano Aran, 50% alpaca, 50% wool (144yds/132m per 100g skein)

2 x 100g skeins in C834 Midnight (dark blue) (M)

Oddment of same or similar yarn in cream (C)

Pair of 5mm (UK6:US8) needles

Pair of 4mm (UK8:US6) needles

Large darning needle

6–8 x buttons ¾in (2cm) in diameter

Tip

Make sure you do not pull the yarn too tightly across the back when working the Fair Isle panels.

Front

Using 5mm needles, M and the cable cast-on method (see page 137), cast on 62 sts.
Work 12 rows in stocking stitch.

Begin pattern:

Join in C and work the 12 rows of the chart using the Fair Isle method (see page 145), working backwards when the centre point is reached.
Break off C and work 10 rows in stocking stitch using M.
Join in C and work the 12 rows of the chart as before.
Break off C and work 10 rows in stocking stitch using M.
Join in C and work the 12 rows of the chart as before.
Break off C and work 12 rows in stocking stitch using M.
Cast off.

Snowflake Chart

Centre point — Right edge

30					25					20					15					10					5					0	Row

☐ Main   ✕ Contrast

Back

Using 5mm needles, M and the cable cast-on method, cast on 62 sts.
Work 9½in (24cm) in stocking stitch.
Change to 4mm needles and work 8 rows in k1, p1 rib.

Flap

Using 5mm needles, M and the cable cast-on method, cast on 62 sts.
Work 5in (12.5cm) in stocking stitch.
Change to 4mm needles and work 2 rows in k1, p1 rib.
Mark position of buttonholes.

Next row (buttonholes): Rib to position of first buttonhole, yf, k2tog; rep along the row until all buttonholes have been worked, then rib to end.

Next row: Rib.
Work 4 further rows in rib.
Cast off in rib.

Making up

Place the cast-on edge of the front and the cast-on edge of the back together, right sides outermost. Pin in place and join by oversewing. Repeat with the cast-off edge of the front and the cast-on edge of the flap. Join sides using mattress stitch (see page 148), overlapping button band appropriately. Attach buttons. Darn in ends.

The cables used for this design are worked in a slightly different way to produce a plaited effect. The luxurious, alpaca-mix yarn makes it really soft and snuggly.

Plaited cables

Sizes
To fit 16[18]in (41[46]cm) cushion pad

Tension
17 sts and 21 rows to 4in (10cm) measured over stocking stitch using 5mm needles.

Materials and equipment
Artesano Aran, 50% alpaca, 50% Peruvian Highland wool (144yds/132m per 100g skein)
3 x 100g skeins in CA03 Maple (cream)
Pair of 5mm (UK6:US8) needles
4mm (UK8:US6) crochet hook
Cable needle
Large darning needle
Large button 1¼in (3cm) in diameter

Abbreviations

C4B = cable 4 sts front: slip next 4 sts on to a cable needle and hold at the back of work; knit next 4 sts, then knit sts from cable needle

C4F = cable 4 sts front: slip next 4 sts on to a cable needle and hold at the front of work; knit next 4 sts, then knit st from cable needle

Ssk = slip the next two stitches, knitwise and individually, to the right needle. Push the left needle from left to right through the front of these stitches and knit them together through the back of the loops

Front

Using the cable cast-on method (see page 137), cast on 78[93] sts.

Row 1: P3, (k12, p3); rep to end.
Row 2: K3, (p12, k3); rep to end.
Row 3: P3, (C4F, k4, p3); rep to end.
Row 4: K3, (p12, k3); rep to end.
Row 5: P3, (k12, p3); rep to end.
Row 6: K3, (p12, k3); rep to end.
Row 7: P3, (k12, p3); rep to end.
Row 8: K3, (p12, k3); rep to end.
Row 9: P3, (k4, C4B, p3); rep to end.
Row 10: K3, (p12, k3); rep to end.
Row 11: P3, (k12, p3); rep to end.
Row 12: K3, (p12, k3); rep to end.
These 12 rows form the pattern. Rep them until work measures 16½[18½]in (42[47]cm).

Shape flap

Keeping to pattern as set and reverting to stocking stitch when it is not possible to work a complete pattern, decrease 1 st at each end of every row thus:

Next row: Ssk, work to last 2 sts, k2tog.
Next row: P2tog, work to last 2 sts, p2togtbl.
Dec thus until there are 22[23] sts on the needles, ending with a purl row.
Next row (buttonhole): Ssk, patt 8 sts, cast off 2[3] sts, patt to last 2 sts, k2tog.
Next row: P2tog, work to cast-off sts, cast on 2[3] sts, work to last 2 sts, p2togtbl.
Dec in this way until there are 6[7] sts on the needle.
Cast off.

Back

Using 5mm needles, cast on 63[71] sts. Work in stocking stitch until work measures 15[17]in (38[43]cm).
Change to smaller needles and work 5 rows in garter stitch.
Cast off.

Making up

Beginning at the side and using a 4mm hook, work a row of double crochet round the edge of the flap to the opposite side edge. If you cannot crochet, work a row of blanket stitch instead. Fold the centre of the shaped edge of flap back to the beginning of the buttonhole and stitch in place for about 1in (2.5cm) on either side of the opening to give a tidy finish. With right side of work outermost, join cast-on edges of front and back by oversewing. Join sides of work as far as flap using mattress stitch (see page 148). Fold flap over and stitch in place. Attach the button to correspond with the buttonhole.

Tip

If the edge of the flap seems too loose, run a gathering thread through the crocheted or blanket-stitched edge to pull it in a little.

Making a circular cover should be a cinch with this ingenious design. It uses a simplified version of short-row shaping that dispenses with tricky wrapped stitches.

In the round

Size

To fit 16in (40cm) circular cushion pad with 2in (5cm) gusset

Tension

15 sts and 22 rows to 4in (10cm) measured over stocking stitch using 5.5mm needles.

Materials and equipment

Wendy Merino Wool Chunky, 100% superwash wool (71yds/65m per 50g ball)
4 x 50g balls in 2476 Damson (purple) (M)
Manos del Uruguay Wool Clasica, 100% handspun wool (138 yds/126m per 100g skein)
1 x 100g skein in 7306 Paris (variegated purples and blues) (C)
Pair of 5.5mm (UK5:US9) needles
Large darning needle
6 x buttons ¾in (2cm) in diameter

KNITTED CUSHIONS

Front

Using 5.5mm needles and M, cast on 30 sts.

Work 2 rows in garter stitch.

Begin to work in pattern.

Pattern

Row 1: K28, turn.

Row 2 and every alternate row: Sl1, k to end.

Row 3: K26, turn.

Row 5: K24, turn.

Row 7: K22, turn.

Cont in this way until the row 'K2, turn' has been worked.

Next row: Sl1, k1.

Next row: K across.

Final row: Sl1, knit to end.

Change to C and rep pattern.

Change to M and rep pattern.

Cont in this way until 12 sections in alternate shades of yarn have been worked.

Cast off.

Back

Work as for front using M for all sections, but do not cast off.

Work a further 2 rows in garter stitch.

Next row (buttonholes): K6, (yf, k2tog, k4); rep instructions in brackets to end.

Work 4 rows in garter stitch.

Cast off.

Making up

Run a gathering thread through the stitches at the centre of the front, pull up tightly and fasten off. Join the cast-on and cast-off stitches of the back to form a complete circle. Omitting the buttonhole band, run a gathering thread through the stitches at the centre of the front, pull up tightly and fasten off. Place the front and back together, right sides outermost. Pin in place, matching shaped sections carefully, and join using the garter stitch

joining technique (see page 149). Take care not to pull the stitches too tightly. Leave the buttonhole band on the back loose until the whole circumference has been joined, then overlap and stitch in place. Stitch the button band in place at the centre back. Attach buttons to correspond with the buttonholes, then attach buttons to the centre back and centre front. Darn in ends.

Put a little love in your life – or someone else's – with this romantic design. The firm knitted fabric can simply be stuffed, so there's no need to search for a special cushion pad.

Heart

Size
Approx 15 x 15in (38 x 38cm)

Tension
15 sts and 29 rows to 4in (10cm) measured over garter stitch using 5mm needles.

Materials and equipment
Manos del Uruguay Silk Blend, 70% wool, 30% silk (150yds/135m per 50g skein)
3 x 50g skeins in 6461 Taurus (variegated reds)
Pair of 5mm (UK6:US8) needles
Cable needle or double-pointed needle
Large darning needle
Good-quality synthetic fibre stuffing

KNITTED CUSHIONS

Abbreviations

Kfb = knit into the front and back of the stitch

C3f = cable 3 sts to the front; slip next 3 sts onto a cable needle or dpn, knit the next 3 sts, then knit the 3 sts from cable needle

Pattern note

This design can be worked with any standard DK yarn held double, or a single strand of any chunky yarn.

Front

Holding yarn double, cast on 3 sts.

Row 1: Knit.

Row 2: Kfb, p to end (4 sts).

Row 3: Kfb, k to end (5 sts).

Row 4: Kfb, p to end (6 sts).

Row 5: Kfb, k to end (7 sts).

Row 6: Kfb, p to end (8 sts).

Row 7 and every foll 10th row: Kfb, C3f across next 6 sts, k1 (9 sts).

Row 8: Kfb, p6, k2 (10 sts).

Row 9: Kfb, k to end (11 sts).

Row 10: Kfb, k1, p6, k3 (12 sts).

Continue thus, increasing at the beginning of every row and working cable on every 10th row until there are 56 sts on the needle.

Keeping cable as set, continue straight until work measures 12in (30cm).

Shape top
Side 1

Row 1: Skpo, k24, k2tog. Place rem 28 sts on stitch holder or spare length of yarn.

Row 2: Knit across (26 sts).

Row 3: Skpo, k to last 2 sts, k2tog (24 sts).

Rep rows 2 and 3 until 18 sts rem.

Now dec 1 st at each end of every row until 8 sts rem.

Cast off.

Side 2

Rejoin yarn to 28 sts left on holder and complete to match side 1.

Back

Work exactly as for front, omitting cable if preferred.

Making up

Beginning at the point of the heart, join one side of cover using mattress stitch. Match top centre points and join across top curves, easing stitches to fit. Join second side of cover from point to halfway up, leaving a gap for inserting stuffing. Using small amounts of stuffing, build up the shape of the 'bumps'. Stuff point, using the end of a knitting needle to push in the stuffing. When you are happy with the shape, stuff the centre of the cushion and close the gap.

Laundry tips

If you need to wash the cushion, do so by hand using a very small amount of good-quality soap powder or liquid handwash detergent. Pat rather than rub and rinse thoroughly. Spin dry or squeeze out as much water as possible and roll in a clean towel. Allow to dry naturally, placing in a warm airing cupboard if possible.

An easy but effective slip stitch pattern and strong contrasts make a cover with rugged good looks. The two back sections are simply overlapped to complete the no-nonsense effect.

Slip stitch check

Size

To fit 16in (41cm) cushion pad

Tension

17 sts and 21 rows to 4in (10cm) measured over stocking stitch using 5mm needles.

Materials and equipment

Artesano Aran, 50% alpaca, 50% Peruvian Highland wool (144yds/132m per 100g skein)
2 x 100g skeins in C850 Mahogany (dark brown) (M)
1 x 100g skein in C810 Ochre (rust) (C)
Pair of 5mm (UK6:US8) knitting needles
Pair of 4mm (UK8:US6) knitting needles
Large darning needle

Abbreviations

Sl1wyb = slip 1 st purlwise with yarn held at back of work

Sl1wyf = slip 1 st purlwise with yarn held at front of work

Pattern note

The pattern uses a multiple of 4 sts + 1 so can easily be adapted to suit any size cushion pad.

Front

Using the cable cast-on method (see page 137), 5mm needles and M, cast on 61[69] sts.

Row 1 (WS): Using M, knit all sts.

Row 2: Using C, (sl1wyb, k3); rep to last st, sl1wyb.

Row 3: Using C, (sl1wyf, k3); rep to last st, sl1wyf.

Row 4: Using M, k2, (sl1wyb, k3); rep to last 3 sts, sl1wyb, k2.

Row 5: Using M, k2, (sl1wyf, k3); rep to last 3 sts, sl1wyf, k2.

Row 6: As row 2.

Row 7: As row 3.

Row 8: Using M, knit all sts.

These 8 rows form the pattern. Rep them until work measures 15[17]in (38[43]cm).

Cast off.

Back (make 2 alike)

Using 5mm needles and M, cast on 61[69] sts and work in stocking stitch for 9½[11]in (24[28]cm).

Change to 4mm needles and work 6 rows in garter stitch.

Cast off loosely.

Making up

With right sides outermost, join cast-on edges of front and one of the back pieces by oversewing. Join cast-off edge of front and cast-on edge of second back piece by oversewing. Join sides of work using mattress stitch (see page 148), overlapping the back pieces appropriately. Darn in the ends.

A striking textured pattern adds interest to the pure wool yarn used for this cover. The crossover method is slightly tricky, but the effect will repay the effort involved.

Cross stitch blocks

Sizes

To fit 16[18]in (41[46]cm) cushion pad

Tension

17 sts and 24 rows to 4in (10cm) measured over stocking stitch using 5mm needles.

Materials and equipment

Jarol Pure British Wool Aran, 100% wool (186yds/170m per ball)

2 x 100g balls in 03 (light brown)

Pair of 5mm (UK6:US8) knitting needles

Pair of 4mm (UK8:US6) knitting needles

Short double-pointed needle (dpn) or cable needle

Large darning needle

7[8] buttons 1in (2.5cm) in diameter

Abbreviations

Sl = slip

Sl1wyb = slip 1 st purlwise with yarn held at back of work

Sl1wyf = slip 1 st purlwise with yarn held at front of work

Front

Using the cable cast-on method (see page 137) and 5mm needles, cast on 66[74] sts.

Rows 1, 3, 5 and 7: Knit all sts.

Rows 2, 4, 6 and 8: (K2, p6); rep to last 2 sts, k2.

Row 9: K7, (sl1wyb, k2, sl1wyb, k4); rep to last 3 sts, k3.

Row 10: K7, (sl1wyf, k2, sl1wyf, k4); rep to last 3 sts, k3.

Row 11: As row 9.

Row 12: As row 10.

Row 13: K7, (sl next 3 sts to dpn and hold at back of work, k1, sl 2 sts from dpn to left needle, take dpn and rem st to front of work, k2 from left needle, k1 from dpn, k4); rep to last 3 sts, k3.

Row 14: As row 2.

These 14 rows form the pattern. Rep them a further 9[10] times.

Work in stocking stitch for 15[17]in (38[43]cm).

Change to smaller needles and work 6 rows in garter stitch.

Cast off.

Flap

With RS of work facing and 4mm needles, pick up and knit 60[67] sts from cast-on edge of front.

Work 6 rows in garter stitch.

Next row (buttonholes): Work until level with first vertical crossed stripe of pattern, yf, k2tog; rep along row so each buttonhole is in line with a vertical crossed stripe.

Work a further 6 rows in garter stitch.

Cast off loosely.

Making up

Pin the sides of cushion in place with the flap overlapping at the back. Join sides using mattress stitch (see page 148). Sew down flap at sides of cover. Attach buttons to correspond with the buttonholes. Darn in ends.

Tip

Check row 13 carefully after working to make sure that the crossed stitches overlap in the same way.

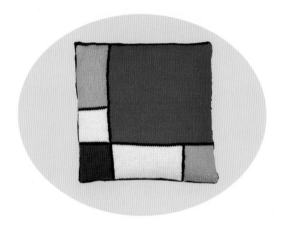

Add a splash of colour to your living room with this bright cushion. Inspired by modern art, it is also the perfect way to use up any oddments of yarn from your stash.

Geometric

Size

To fit 18in (46cm) cushion pad

Tension

17 sts and 21 rows to 4in (10cm) measured over stocking stitch using 4.5mm needles.

Materials and equipment

Aran-weight wool or wool-mix yarn

4 x 50g balls in main colour (black) (A)

About 40g of first contrast colour (red) (B)

Oddments of similar yarn in yellow (C), cream (D) and blue (E)

Pair of 4.5mm (UK7:US7) needles

Pair of 4mm (UK8:US6) needles

Large darning needle

4–8 buttons

Pattern notes

This made good use of my stash, including oddments of red and yellow Artesano Aran and a scrap of unknown blue yarn. I also found some black Debbie Bliss Chunky that knitted to an Aran gauge, and used a ball of cream Jaeger Matchmaker DK double.

Instructions are given from the top down; the design is intended to be displayed with the red square at the top right.

Special instructions

This cover is worked using intarsia (see page 145). Use separate balls of each colour and do not carry the yarn across the back of the work.

Method

Wind off about 2yds (2m) of yarn A, then make a loop and cast on 74 sts using the cable cast-on method (see page 137).

Row 1: Knit.

Row 2: Purl.

Row 3: Knit, working 2A, 17C, 1A, 52B, 2A.

Row 4: Purl, working 2A, 52B, 1A, 17C, 2A.

Rep the last 2 rows 22 times, twisting all three strands of yarn together at the C/A/B colour change to prevent gaps. Work should measure approx 8in (20cm) from cast-on edge. Break off C.

Next row: Knit, working 20A, 52B, 2A.

Next row: Purl, working 2A, 52B, 20A.

Next row: Knit, joining in D as appropriate and working 2A, 17D, 1A, 52B, 2A.

Next row: Purl, working 2A, 52B, 1A, 17D, 2A.

Rep last 2 rows 10 times. Work should measure approx 12in (30cm) from cast-on edge. Break off D and B.

Next row: Using A, knit.

Next row: Using A, purl.

Next row: Knit, working 2A, 17E, 1A, 34D, 1A, 17C, 2A.

Next row: Purl, working 2A, 17C, 1A, 34D, 1A, 17E, 2A.

Rep last 2 rows 10 times.

Work 2 rows in A.

Cast off.

Back

Using A and the cable cast-on method, cast on 74 sts.

Row 1: Knit.

Row 2: Purl.

Rep the last 2 rows until work measures 12in (30cm).

Change to 4mm needles and work 6 rows in garter st.

Cast off in rib.

Back flap

Using A and the cable cast-on method, cast on 74 sts.

Row 1: Knit.

Row 2: Purl.

Rep the last 2 rows until work measures 5in (13cm).

Change to 4mm needles and work 2 rows in 2 x 2 rib.

Mark desired position of buttonholes and work following instructions on page 147.

Work 3 further rows in rib.

Cast off in rib.

Tip

If you have no chunky yarn in the shade you want, make your own by using two strands of double knitting.

Making up

Press work very lightly avoiding rib. Place cast-on edges of back and front together and join by oversewing from the outside, matching stitches carefully. Join sides to end of ribbing using mattress stitch (see page 148). Join cast-on edge of flap to cast-off edge of front by oversewing. Join sides, overlapping ribbing and sewing down firmly. Attach buttons to correspond with buttonholes.

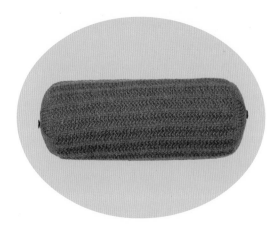

This shape of cushion is perfect for the small of your back, but it's difficult to find a suitable cover. This simple fancy rib design ensures a snug fit, while shaped ends give a tailored look.

Bolster

Size

To fit a 16in (41cm) bolster with 6in (15cm)-wide ends and a diameter of approx 18½in (47cm)

Tension

16 sts and 24 rows to 4in (10cm) measured over stocking stitch using 5mm needles.

Materials

Artesano Aran, 50% alpaca, 50% wool (144yds/132m per 100g skein)
2 x 100g skeins in C810 Ochre
Pair of 5mm (UK6:US8) knitting needles
Large darning needle
2 small buttons (optional)

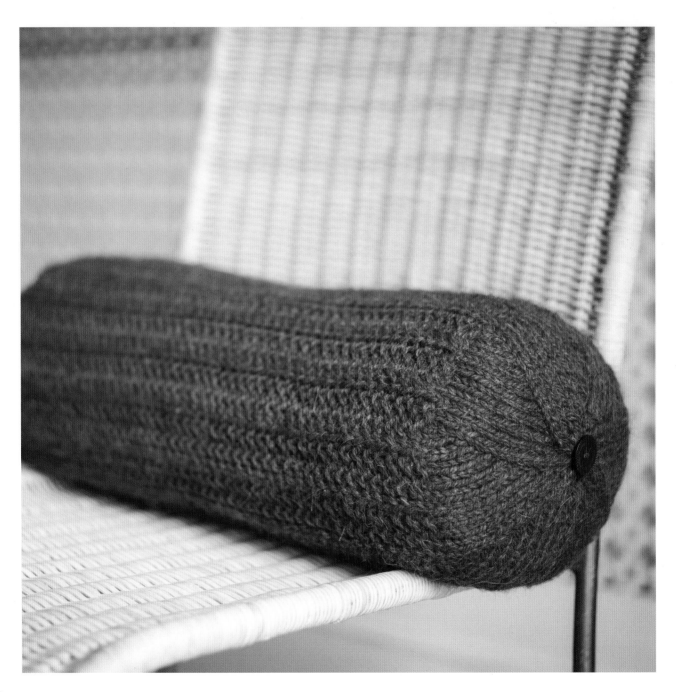

KNITTED CUSHIONS

Bolster

Using 5mm needles, cast on 69 sts and work in mistake rib pattern:

Row 1: (K2, p2); rep to last st, k1.

Rep this row until work measures 15½in (39.5cm).

End shaping

Row 1: Knit, casting on 1 st at end of row (70 sts).

Row 2 and every alt row: Purl.

Row 3: (K8, k2tog) to end (63 sts).

Row 5: (K7, k2tog) to end (56 sts).

Row 7: (K6, k2tog) to end (49 sts).

Cont in this way until the row '(k1, k2tog) to end' has been worked.

Thread yarn through rem sts. Fasten off.

Second end

Pick up and knit 70 sts from cast-on edge.

Beginning with row 2, complete second end to match first.

Making up

Match the open portion of the ends carefully and join as far as the top of the sides using mattress stitch (see page 148). Place pad in cover and, still using mattress stitch, join the side seam. Darn in loose ends of yarn. Attach buttons if desired.

Making the cushion bigger

Bolster circumference	Sts to cast on	Stitch count for ends
19–21in (48.5–53.5cm)	77	77
22–23in (56–58.5cm)	85	84 (dec 1 st)
24–25in (61–63.5cm)	91	91

Variation

If your bolster is bigger than the example used in this pattern, it is easy to work out how to make a cover. Measure its circumference and refer to the chart to work out how many stitches to cast on. Work the sides to an appropriate length, then follow the instructions for extra decrease rows below.

Extra decrease rows:

From 91 sts: (K11, k2tog) to end (84 sts).

From 84 sts: (K10, k2tog) to end (77 sts).

From 77 sts: (K9, k2tog) to end (70 sts).

Tip

If you want to be able to remove the cover, use nylon press fasteners to close the last third of the long seam.

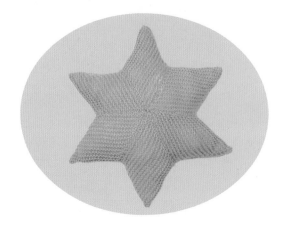

Joined parallelograms make a really effective star shape. If you want to make a bigger star-shaped cushion, follow the same method in the instructions but use larger needles and chunky yarn.

Star

Size

The finished cushion measures about 17in (43cm) from point to point made in Aran-weight yarn using 4.5mm needles, or about 20in (51cm) from point to point made in chunky yarn using 5.5mm needles.

Tension

16 sts and 22 rows to 4in (10cm) measured over stocking stitch using 4.5mm needles.

Materials and equipment

Drops Alaska, 100% wool (77yds/70m per 50g ball)
3 x 50g balls in 58 Mustard
Pair of 4.5mm (UK7:US7) knitting needles
Quantity of stuffing
Large darning needle

Pattern note

When picking up stitches you may find it easier to use a needle a size smaller.

Front and back (make 2 pieces alike)

Using the cable cast-on method (see page 137), cast on 22 sts.

Row 1: Knit.

Row 2: Inc in first st, k to last 2 sts, k2tog.

Row 3: Knit.

Rep rows 2 and 3 a further 13 times (14 ridges, forming a slant to the right). Cast off 21 sts, leaving 1 st on the needle.

Working from this stitch, pick up and knit a further 21 sts down the left side of the parallelogram.

Rep from Row 1 to form a second parallelogram.

Cont in this way until 6 sections of the star have been worked.

Cast off.

Make a second piece in exactly the same way.

Making up

Place the two sections of the star together, right sides outermost, and pin together. Join by oversewing the edges, matching the points carefully. When all but one side has been joined, stuff the star shape very firmly, using the end of a large knitting needle to push the stuffing into the points. Close the last side by oversewing.

Tip

Emptying a cheap 16in (41cm) synthetic cushion pad will provide sufficient filling and will probably be cheaper than buying the equivalent amount of bagged stuffing.

A naked cushion!

Techniques

First things first

Before you start knitting any of the projects in this book, there are a few things to decide first. If you are planning to revamp your existing cushions, all you need to do is remove the old covers and check that the pads are still in good condition. If you are starting from scratch and need to buy new pads, the guide below will help you to choose the perfect foundation for your project.

Cushion sizes

Decide what size cushion you need. They come in all shapes and sizes, but the two most common are about 16in (41cm) and 18in (46cm) square. If you want something larger, try the bedding section of a department store: a 24in (61cm) square or a 'continental' pillow would make a fabulous floor cushion.

For plump, inviting, well-filled cushions, buy a pad a little larger than the cover. Don't worry about whether it will fit, because knitting is stretchy. To revamp existing cushions, remove and measure the pads, then make the new covers 1–2in (2.5–5cm) smaller.

Cushion pads

Various fillings are available, but, as with most things in life, you usually get what you pay for. A cheap cushion pad will soon go flat or lumpy. Feather or feather and down pads are best, although if you are worried about allergies some good synthetic substitutes are available. Pads are also available by mail order or online.

Tension

The tension or gauge is the number of stitches needed to produce a given measurement, usually 4 x 4in (10 x 10cm) square. For a professional result, it is essential to check your tension; a small difference can have a big impact on the size of the finished cover. For cushions that will take a lot of wear, it is best to work to a tighter tension than suggested on the ball band.

Working a tension swatch

If you are a new knitter, begin a habit that will pay dividends: work a tension swatch before you begin each project. This will help you to learn your natural tension, and you will be far less likely to waste expensive yarn. Keep the labelled swatches for future reference.

Cast on the number of stitches that the pattern advises will produce 4in (10cm) in width, plus two more stitches. Work for the number of rows given to produce 4in (10cm) in length, plus two more rows. Cast off and press lightly, unless the ball band of your yarn suggests otherwise. Measure the square each way, one stitch inside the edge. If it is smaller or larger than 4in (10cm), try again with larger or smaller needles.

Guide to number of stitches per 4in (10cm)

Yarn	4ply	DK (light)	DK (standard)	Aran	Chunky	Super-chunky
Sts to 4in (10cm)	28	24	22	20	18–20	7–10

Materials and equipment

You don't need anything complicated for making cushion covers, just a few balls of yarn and one or two pairs of needles. Here are some tips that will help you to make the right choices before you begin knitting.

Needles and hooks

The designs in this book are worked using standard straight needles. These come in a wide range of materials, including metal, plastic and bamboo. Metal is the most durable but can feel cold. Plastic is often used for larger needles, but the points may be blunter and more difficult to insert. Bamboo needles are very smooth, and help to prevent snags when using rough-textured yarn. Double-pointed needles are useful for working cables or i-cord.

If you know how, crochet hooks can be used for joining or for working decorative edging stitches.

Yarn

Many types of yarn are available, but for cushions that wash and wear well, buy the best you can afford. Wool always looks good, but choose 'superwash' wool if you want to wash your cover. A wool-mix yarn may be more durable. Cashmere or alpaca is soft and luxurious but is expensive. Fluffy or novelty yarns can be effective, but may not last as long. Cotton or bamboo yarn produces a firm, long-lasting fabric that will survive repeated laundering.

Substituting yarn

This is relatively straightforward, but never rely on the ball band; one manufacturer's double knitting, Aran or chunky may be very different from another's. If the ball length is similar, the yarn is likely to knit to a similar tension. If the length per ball is very different, the yarn itself may be thicker or thinner. Balls of yarn made from a different fibre or combination of fibres may be shorter or longer than the recommended yarn, so you may need more – or if you're lucky, fewer – balls.

Combining yarn

If you cannot find the right shade of yarn in the weight you need, try combining strands to make up your own yarn. This is also a good way of using up yarn oddments. As a rough guide, two strands of 3-ply equal one strand of double knitting, two strands of 4-ply equal one strand of Aran, and two strands of double knitting equal one strand of chunky yarn. Whichever yarn you choose, make sure you work to the tension given in the pattern. Remember that if you want your work to look exactly the same as the illustration, you must use the recommended yarn.

Joining yarn

Never join yarn mid-row as a knot will spoil the look of your work. Even if you split the strands and twist the ends together, it will never be as strong as unbroken yarn. Join the yarn a stitch in from the beginning of the row, working the first stitch with a strand from the new ball and the previous ball held together. As a rough guide, there will be enough yarn to work a row if the length remaining measures roughly twice the width of the work.

Knitting techniques

Over the next few pages we survey the basic knitting techniques you will need to be familiar with to tackle the projects in this book.

Simple cast-on

1 Form a slip knot on the left needle. Insert the right needle into the loop and wrap the yarn around it as shown.

2 Pull the yarn through the first loop to create a new one.

3 Slide the new loop onto the left needle and continue in this way until you have the required number of stitches.

Cable cast-on

1 For a firmer edge, cast on the first two stitches as shown (right).

2 When casting on the third and subsequent stitches, insert needle between cast-on stitches on left needle, wrap yarn round and pull through to create a loop. Slide loop onto left needle. Repeat to end.

Thumb method cast-on

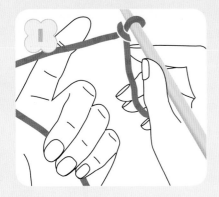

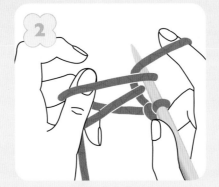

1 Leaving a long end, make a slip knot. Place on the needle and pull tight. Hold the needle and the yarn end in the right hand.

2 Wrap the yarn round the left thumb from front to back. Push the needle point through the thumb loop from front to back. Wind the yarn around the needle from left to right.

3 Pull the yarn loop through the thumb loop, remove thumb and pull tight, using the yarn end. Repeat until the desired number of stitches are on the needle.

Casting off

1 Knit two stitches, then slip the first stitch over the second and let it drop off the needle.

2 Knit another stitch so there are two stitches on needle. Repeat steps 1 and 2 until one stitch remains. Break yarn and thread through remaining stitch.

Casting off in rib

Keep rib pattern by knitting or purling stitches as appropriate when casting off.

Knit stitch

1 Hold the needle with the cast-on stitches in your left hand. Place the tip of the right needle into the first stitch and wrap the yarn round.

2 Pull the yarn through to create a new loop.

3 Slip the newly made stitch onto the right needle. Continue in the same way for each stitch on the left-hand needle. To start a new row, turn the work to swap the needles and repeat steps 1–3.

Purl stitch

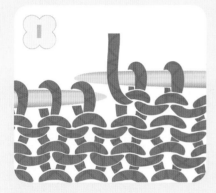

1 Hold the yarn at the front of the work as shown.

2 Place the right needle into the first stitch from front to back. Wrap the yarn around the needle in an anti-clockwise direction as shown.

3 Bring the needle back through the stitch and pull through.

Stitch variations

A Garter stitch

Knit every row.

B Stocking stitch

Knit on RS rows and purl on WS rows.

C Moss stitch

With an even number of stitches:
Row 1: (K1, p1) to end.
Row 2: (P1, k1) to end.
Rep rows 1 and 2 for pattern.

With an odd number of stitches:
Row 1: * K1, p1; rep from * to last stitch, k1.
Rep to form pattern.

D Single (1 x 1) rib

With an even number of stitches:
Row 1: *K1, p1; * rep to end.
Rep for each row.

With an odd number of stitches:
Row 1: *K1, p1, rep from * to last stitch, k1.
Row 2: *P1, k1, rep from * to last stitch, p1.

E Double (2 x 2) rib

Row 1: *K2, p2; rep from * to end.
Rep for each row.

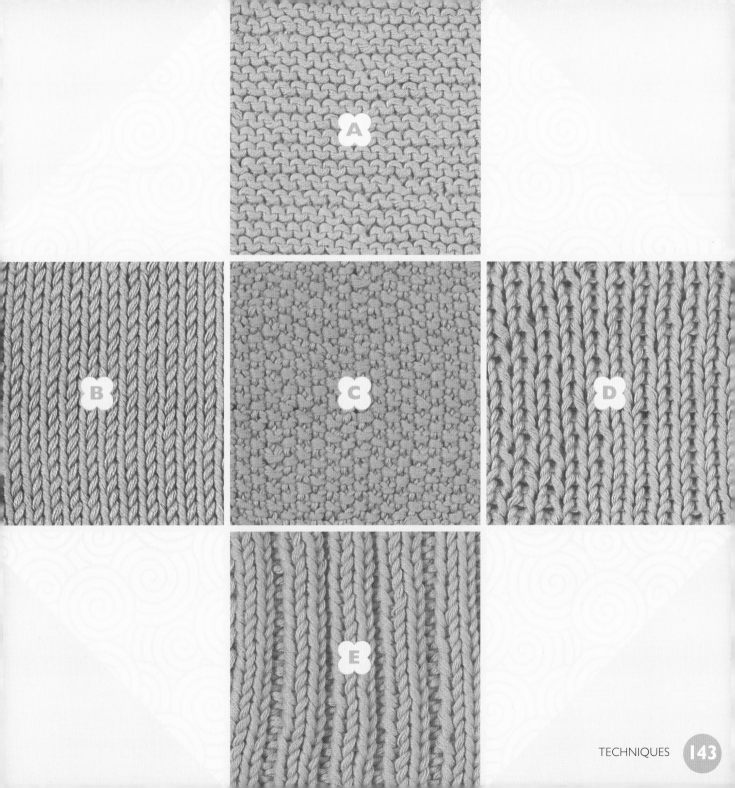

Cable stitch

With the help of a cable needle, these decorative stitches are quite straightforward. Stitches are slipped onto the needle and then knitted later to create the twists.

Front cable worked over 4 stitches

1 Slip the next 2 sts onto a cable needle and hold in front of work.

2 Knit the next 2 sts from the left needle as normal, then knit the 2 sts from the cable needle.

Back cable worked over 4 stitches

Slip the next 2 sts onto a cable needle and hold at back of work.

Knit the next 2 sts from the left needle as normal, then knit the 2 sts from the cable needle.

Colour knitting

This book features a number of colourwork projects, for which you will need to use either the Fair Isle or the intarsia technique for changing colours.

Fair Isle

Intarsia

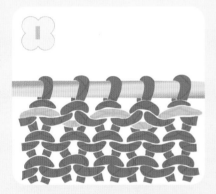

This is worked by picking up or setting aside different shades of yarn as needed. Yarn that is not in use is stranded or carried across the back of the row. Twist each shade of yarn every few stitches, and take care not to pull the yarn too tightly across the back of the work.

1 Begin working with the first shade, then drop it when you need to use the second. To work with the first shade again, bring it under the second.

2 When picking up the second shade again, drop the first and take the second over it.

Unlike Fair Isle, this is worked in blocks using separate balls of yarn for each colour. Twist yarns at each colour change to prevent gaps. Yarn is not carried across the back of the work so there is no risk of puckering.

Fastenings

If you are sure you will never want to remove your cushion cover for laundering, just make the front and back the same size, then sew the pad into it. A flap that is simply folded over like a pillowslip without fastening is also an option. Otherwise, you will need to decide how to fasten your work.

Buttons

Attractive buttons can be a real feature, so it's worth searching for the right ones to complement your work. Use as many as you like to achieve the desired effect, following the guide below on how to place and work buttonholes. For finer yarn such as double knitting, use up to eight smaller buttons. For thicker yarn, fewer and bigger buttons will probably look better.

Buttonholes

These are usually made over one or two stitches, depending on yarn thickness and button size. Make sure they are large enough for the chosen buttons to pass through and if necessary work a test buttonhole first. Buttonholes that gape can be adjusted by sewing a tiny stitch at each side.

Placing buttonholes

Work the flap to where you want to place the buttons. Using contrasting yarn, mark the position of each buttonhole one row below, then work the buttonhole row.

Buttonhole over one stitch

Row 1: Work to marker, yarn forward (or leave yarn at front); knit two stitches together. Repeat to last buttonhole; work to end of row.
Row 2: Work across, treating each 'yf' as a stitch.

Buttonhole over two stitches

Row 1: Work to one stitch before marker; turn work and cast off two stitches, turn and work to position of next buttonhole. Repeat to last buttonhole; work to end of row.
Row 2: Work to gap, turn and cast on two stitches, turn and work to next gap. Repeat to last buttonhole; work to end of row.

Alternative fastenings

If you are daunted by button-holes, there are several ways to cheat. The easiest is to sew hook-and-eye tape dots or press fasteners at intervals along the flap. Decorative buttons can be added to the outside of the flap, positioned over the dots or press fasteners.

Some knitters prefer to set a zip fastener into the side of a cushion, or to make the back of the cover in two halves with a zip in the middle. This can be quite tricky, so is best left to those who are handy with a sewing needle.

Sewing up

Once you have knitted the pieces for your cushion cover you will need to join them. Careful making up can make all the difference to a knitted piece, so take your time to create a professional-looking finish.

Oversewing

With wrong sides of work together, insert the needle from back to front through both pieces, slanting the needle from right to left. Pull through. Insert the needle from the back, just behind where the thread is emerging and, slanting the needle as before, bring it through to the front.

Mattress stitch

Place the pieces to be joined on a flat surface laid together side by side, with right sides towards you. Using matching yarn, thread a needle back and forth with small, straight stitches. The stitches form a ladder between the two pieces of fabric, creating a flat, secure seam.

Garter stitch joins

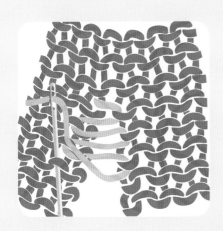

It is easy to join garter stitch as it has a firm edge and lies flat. Place the edges of the work together, right side up, and see where the stitches line up. Pick up the bottom loops of the stitches on one side of the work and the top loops of the stitches on the other side.

After a few stitches, pull gently on the yarn. The stitches should lock together and lie completely flat. The inside of the join should look the same as it does on the outside.

Backstitch

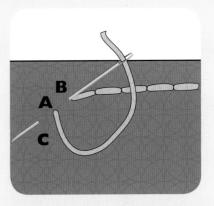

Make a knot to secure yarn at back of work. Bring the needle up to point A, insert at point B, and bring back up at point C. Repeat, keeping the stitches an even length.

Finishing touches

As cushions are usually square or rectangular, they are easy to adapt to your requirements. If you want a patterned back rather than a plain one, a different flap, or garter stitch rather than ribbing, just do it. The size can be adjusted by consulting the tension and adding or subtracting stitches appropriately.

Added detail can also help to make your cushions striking and unique. If you are not very good at sewing up, try working blanket stitch over a messy edge: it will hide a multitude of sins.

Blanket stitch

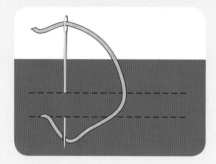 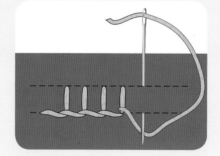

Work from left to right. The twisted edge should lie on the outer edge of the fabric to form a raised line. Bring needle up at point A, down at B and up at C with thread looped under the needle. Pull through. Take care to tighten the stitches equally. Repeat to the right. Fasten the last loop by taking a small stitch along the lower line.

Making a tassel

1 Cut a piece of stiff card so the height is the required length of your tassel. Wrap the yarn around it several times, depending on how full you require the tassel to be. Secure this bundle with a separate length of yarn threaded through at one end and tied to leave long ends. Cut through the bundle at the opposite end.

2 Keeping the strands folded in half, remove the card. About a quarter of the way down from the fold, wind a separate length of yarn a few times around the whole bundle, including the long ends of the tie, to form the head of the tassel. Tie the two ends of this length of yarn together tightly. Trim all the ends of yarn at the base of the tassel to give a tidy finish.

Abbreviations

alt	alternate
approx	approximately
beg	beginning
ch	chain
cm	centimetre(s)
cn	cable needle
cont	continue
dec	decrease
DK	double knitting
dpn	double-pointed needle
foll	following
g	gram
in	inch(es)
inc	increase by working into front, then back of stitch
inc1	increase by working into front and back of stitch
k	knit
kfb	knit into front and back of stitch
k-wise	with needles positioned as for working a knit stitch
k1b	knit into the back of the stitch
k2tog	knit two stitches together

m	metre(s)
M1	make one stitch by picking up the strand of yarn between the last stitch worked and the next stitch and knitting into the back of it
MB	make bobble: knit into front, back, front then back again of next stitch, turn; sl1, p3, turn; sl1, k3, turn; (p2tog) twice, turn; skpo
mm	millimetre(s)
p	purl
patt	pattern
p2tog	purl two stitches together
P3tog WTO	purl three stitches together without taking them off the needle
p-wise	with needles positioned as for a purl stitch
psso	pass slipped stitch over
rem	remaining
rep	repeat
RS	right side of work
rev st st	reverse stocking stitch
skpo	slip one, knit one, pass slipped stitch over
sl1	slip a stitch as though to knit it
sl1 p-wise	slip the next stitch by inserting needle from right to left

sll wyb	slip one stitch with yarn held at the back of the work
ss	slip stitch
ssk	slip next two stitches, knitwise and individually, to the right needle. Push the left needle through the front of these sts from left to right and knit them together through the back loops
sssk	slip next three stitches, knitwise and one at a time, to the right needle. Push the left needle through the front of these stitches from left to right, then knit them together (two stitches decreased)
st(s)	stitch(es)
st st	stocking stitch
tbl	through the back of the loop
tog	together
wyb	with yarn held at the back of the work
WS	wrong side of work
yb	yarn back
yds	yards
yf	yarn forward
yrn	wrap yarn completely round needle
*	work instructions following * then repeat as directed

UK/US yarn weights

UK	US
4-ply	Sport
Double knitting	Light worsted
Aran	Fisherman/worsted
Chunky	Bulky

Knitting needle sizes

UK	Metric	US
13	2.25mm	1
12	2.75mm	2
10	3.25mm	3
–	3.5mm	4
9	3.75mm	5
8	4mm	6
7	4.5mm	7
6	5mm	8
5	5.5mm	9
4	6mm	10
3	6.5mm	10.5
2	7mm	10.5
1	7.5mm	11

About the author

Alison Howard has been knitting since she was nine years old. A former journalist, she worked as a magazine editor before becoming a book editor. She now works mainly as a freelance editor in the craft sector, as well as editing and checking knitting and crochet patterns, and proofreading and editing academic theses. Alison has edited books in GMC's 'Cozy' series, has written *Knitted & Crocheted Slippers* and *Mug Hugs*, and co-authored *Tea Cozies 3*. She has also been a consultant or written under a 'house' name for various other titles, including *Your Tudor Homework Helper*, *Your Victorian Homework Helper*, *Extreme Machines* and *Amazing Inventions*.

Acknowledgements

GMC Publications would like to thank Emma Foster for photographic styling.

Suppliers

Artesano Ltd
Unit G, Lambs Farm
Business Park
Basingstoke Road
Swallowfield
Reading
Berkshire
RG7 1PQ
Tel: +44 (0)118 9503350
www.artesanoyarns.co.uk

Debbie Bliss
Designer Yarns Ltd
Unit 8–10
Newbridge Industrial Estate
Pitt Street
Keighley
West Yorkshire
BD21 4PQ
Tel: +44 (0)1535 664222
www.designeryarns.uk.com

Coats Crafts UK
Green Lane Mill
Holmfirth
West Yorkshire
HD9 2DX
Tel: +44 (0)1481 681881
www.coatscrafts.co.uk

Manos del Uruguay
www.manosyarns.com

Sirdar Spinning Ltd
Flanshaw Lane
Wakefield
West Yorkshire
WF2 9ND
Tel: +44 (0)1924 371501
www.sirdar.co.uk

Wool Warehouse
ww.woolwarehouse.co.uk

Index

To place an order, or to request a catalogue, contact:

GMC Publications Ltd

Castle Place, 166 High Street, Lewes, East Sussex, BN7 1XU

United Kingdom

Tel: +44 (0)1273 488005

Website: www.gmcbooks.com